FOOD FOR THE SOUL

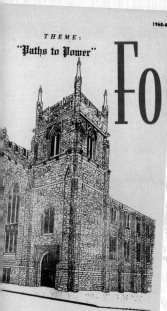

THEME: "Paths to Power"

1960-61

YSSINIAN BAPTIST CHURCH
"The Church of the Masses"
NEW YORK 30, N. Y.   AUDUBON 6-2626
David N. Licorish   Oberia D. Dempsey
ASSOCIATE MINISTERS

FOOD FOR THE SOUL

Recipes and Stories from the Congregation of
Harlem's Abyssinian Baptist Church

One World • Ballantine Books
New York

No book can replace the diagnostic expertise and medical advice of a trusted physician. Please be certain to consult with your doctor before making any decisions that affect your health, particularly if you suffer from any medical condition or have any symptom that may require treatment.

Published in the United States by One World Books, an imprint of The Random House Publishing Group, a division of Random House, Inc., New York.

ONE WORLD is a registered trademark and the One World colophon is a trademark of Random House, Inc.

All of the individual stories and recipes in this collection are reprinted courtesy of the members and friends of The Abyssinian Baptist Church of New York.

All photographs courtesy of The Abyssinian Baptist Church and its members unless otherwise noted.

Credits and permissions can be found on p. 269.

Library of Congress Cataloging-in-Publication Data
    Food for the soul : recipes and stories from the congregation of Harlem's Abyssinian Baptist Church.
        p.   cm.
    ISBN 0-345-47621-2
    1. African American cookery.   2. Cookery, American—Southern style.
I. Mattison, Booker T.   II. Abyssinian Baptist Church (New York, N.Y.)

TX715.F6785 2005
641.59'296073—dc22   2005040857

Printed in the United States of America

www.oneworldbooks.net

9 8 7 6 5 4 3 2 1

Book design by Mercedes Everett

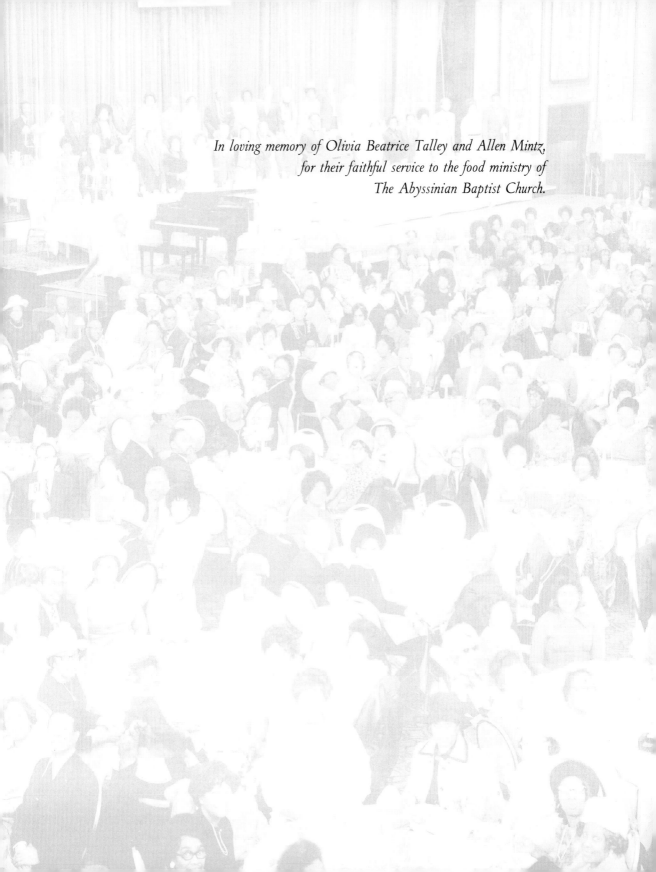

*In loving memory of Olivia Beatrice Talley and Allen Mintz,
for their faithful service to the food ministry of
The Abyssinian Baptist Church.*

Nehemiah said,
"Go and enjoy choice food and sweet drinks,
and send some to those who have nothing prepared.
This day is sacred to our Lord. Do not grieve,
for the joy of the Lord is your strength."

—Nehemiah 8:10 (NIV)

Foreword

Carole Darden-Lloyd and husband, Edward Lloyd,
worshipping at Abyssinian.

I am awed by how God consistently granted our forbearers the spiritual and physical strength necessary to survive capture in Africa, months spent languishing in slave castles, the demeaning conditions of the Middle Passage, and the brutality of American slavery. In Africa, anything devoted to the soul and the spirit usually involved the communal sharing of food. Once we arrived in America an adaptation of this ritual was made because we only could get what we were given. The slaves who worked in the field had one type of exposure and creativity, and those who worked in the house had another. The result of these two experiences was not only a stroke of culinary genius called soul food, but a significant contribution to the elevation of American cuisine, made while toiling in "Massa's" kitchen and surviving on his scraps. The church was the main institution to carry along our culinary expertise through various church functions, and through the tradition of feeding the preacher.

The clues to understanding how we have survived as a people can be found in our understanding of our spiritual history. This history is so extraordinary, and our ability to have survived on this planet such a magnificent feat, that it is despairing to me how disconnected some of us are from it. I try to incorporate that extraordinary history as a source of guidance and strength on a daily basis, and attending Abyssinian Baptist Church has helped me further the connection to those spiritual roots. I didn't start going back to church until my husband felt the need to do so almost fifteen years ago. I was looking for a church for him when I found Abyssinian Baptist Church. He went first, and once I began attending I realized how much I needed to tap into this spiritual heritage. Abyssinian spoke to me, and to all of my childhood experiences in church in the South—the historic Baptist preacher as embodied by Reverend Calvin Butts; black voices raised in song; gospel music, so expressive of our energy; and spirituals, simply the most miraculous body of religious music ever composed. I can't conceive of any other race of people so robust to survive all that we have endured—it speaks volumes about the quality of the spirit of our people.

Cooking was always recreational for my sister, Norma Jean, and me, so after school or on weekends we would cook with our mother. It might only be some sort of small treat, but nonetheless it was our ritual in the kitchen together. My parents were older when they married, so we were surrounded by an older family. All of those women, and the men, too, cooked. They understood that this was a valuable role. Not only was this a role that provided nourishment, but it also established the discipline of the day. Breakfast occurred at a specific hour, lunch at another, and dinner at still another. Everything accommodated work and family time in almost equal measure of importance. If someone was working a long hard day, the one time they would really commune with family was around the breakfast or dinner table. And breakfast was really serious in our family. To this day I wouldn't think of leaving the house without having breakfast. You don't really know when your next meal will be, and it is impossible to know what the day will bring. So this continues to be a rule in our household.

I fear that the ritual of daily coming together around food is in danger of being lost. Except for special occasions, families are eating at different times, and some don't sit down to eat at all. These habits aren't beneficial because one loses the advantage of communing with family and all of the important communication that comes with that. Unquestionably, matters of health get lost when less attention is paid to what, when, and how we eat.

The older I get, the more time I need for personal reflection. This is why cooking is a hobby for me—it brings some spiritual relief into my work day.

Even though cooking involves creating and accomplishing a goal for my family and me, it also allows for a certain amount of personal reflection. Through cooking you can re-create in meaningful ways and become more disciplined in every aspect of your life as a result. I have certainly done that through food. The more I do it, the easier it becomes, and, if you keep doing it, your own magic starts to develop, because practice makes perfect. Your own self will translate into your meals, even if what you cook is not exactly what you take from a recipe.

A dear friend and mentor, Carrie Carter, was in her eighties when she showed my sister and me how to make our now famous tea sandwiches. Carrie ran a catering business in Montclair, New Jersey, for many, many years. While she was making these sandwiches, she recounted her entire life, which at times was very difficult. She had been married three times, widowed twice, and one husband ran off with a younger woman. She had lost her only child, an adult daughter, who had worked with her in her catering business. As she was recounting all of this, she did so with such serenity and equanimity. All of these terrible things had happened to her, but it was just a life, and she had lived it. She had survived. She had accepted it. And part of how she triumphed was in the making of these sandwiches. She said that the rhythm of making her sandwiches brought great joy and pleasure. Carrie was talking about that skill, that routine, that discipline, that transcends your circumstances and becomes such a part of you that it evolves into a comforting and consoling rhythm of life. We can all learn this from Carrie Carter, because if we live life the way it's mapped out right now where life is work, work, work; grab a bite; sleep; work, work, work just to stay above water, it becomes increasingly difficult to find relief and reflect on the goodness of God.

Everyone should view cooking as a hobby, since it has to be done anyway. Even if it starts as hard work, with discipline it can become one of your rhythms of life. We are all familiar with that rhythm whether we realize it or not. Just think back to people who have made cooking look so easy and effortless. But if you buy into the marketing industry's pitches that it is much easier to eat prepared foods, then you've already entered into the category of the insecure cook. You're either convinced that it's too hard and you can't do it, or it takes too much time to think about. True, it does take some thoughtfulness, and the thoughtfulness requires discipline. There are no easy fixes. But the rewards on the other side are that you are able to nourish yourself and your family, and you can take pride in that role as you express concern over your own health and the health of your family. It takes a little longer, but it's healthier, so that's the route we should take. A strong body is crucial to a sound spiritual life. You can't have one without the other, so you owe it to yourself to enhance that spirituality through a strong body.

When our book *Spoonbread and Strawberry Wine* was reissued, a couple of reviews expressed disappointment that some of the recipes were not adapted to a more healthy way of cooking. But our book wasn't supposed to be a health book. It was a historical reference of our family, and to change that would have altered that history. And the irony is that our relatives were not obese. We didn't snack in between meals. On the rare occasion that we were offered a snack, it was a piece of fruit or a special treat at night. In the South I remember that treat being shaved ice with pieces of pineapple and a little pineapple syrup. We also adhered to activity and work. We played outside and, unfortunately, that is a luxury for children today. Women who stayed at home would work all the day long. We weren't organized around a television. But most important, everything was fresh and cooked from scratch. Prepared foods, processed in factories and laden with salt, sugar, and chemical additives were simply not available. It is important to understand that the epidemic rise in chronic diseases such as obesity and heart disease has occurred in the context of the growth of the prepared food industry. It's inescapable! You are what you eat.

In the black church we strategize on what to do about the multitude of sins that affect our community, such as schools that are failing our children and the breakdown of the family structure. We need to approach matters of health in the same way. We can no longer remain silent about the unhealthy food choices that are silently killing us. Many Negro spirituals refer to Christian soldiers on the battlefield for the Lord. We have to start viewing our health as the next battlefield. We have proven throughout the ages that we can survive almost anything, and though this enemy of an unhealthy diet is insidious, we must go after it with the same vehemence that we've gone after other social and political issues.

Food preparation is always a loving gesture. The very nature of wanting to prepare a healthful meal and give it to someone else is an act of love because in nourishing the body you certainly nourish the soul. Both the person who prepares the food and the person who receives it are enhanced. Food also connects us to the physical world and reminds us to be grateful because we recognize the blessing of having something so crucial to our survival. Of all the things that are necessary to life, food is the one that is constantly acknowledged. We rarely thank God for our clothes before we dress, and we don't usually give thanks for shelter before we leave home. But thank God that as a people we have preserved the ritual of saying grace, the giving of thanks before meals that we lovingly share with one another. The creation of this cookbook is an extension of that love.

Carole Darden-Lloyd,
co-author, *Spoonbread and Strawberry Wine*,
Harlem, New York, 2005

Acknowledgments

Thanks be to God for guiding The Abyssinian Baptist Church ministry into the publishing arena. We pray that this work will allow you to experience the joys of soulful cooking and healthy living. We also praise God for our ancestors who created soul food and passed down the spirit of soul-filled cooking as an enduring tradition to share with family and friends from generation to generation.

A project of this scope is the handiwork of many people, some were contributors and others worked diligently behind the scenes. The heart of this work is in the varied recipes that come from the many traditions found among our congregation. Throughout this collection of delectable food ideas, you will find that a number of dishes were handed down through generations while others offer a modern twist on style and dietary practices.

We must further thank the Abyssinian Deacons, Deaconesses, Trustees, congregation, and friends for supporting of this project with recipes or editorial input. Special thanks to Bob Gore, chairman of the Abyssinian Trustee Board, for providing impetus for this project, and for his astute insight and key liaison work between the publisher and The Abyssinian Baptist Church. Moreover, this cookbook could not have been completed without the professional oversight of

Dr. Anita Underwood and Naomi Graham, who tediously combed through every element of text to bring this work to a stage of fruition.

Thanks to Scott Waxman, a wonderful literary agent who first approached us with the cookbook concept. His creative and marketing savvy have been central to the whole undertaking.

Much gratitude is due to our editor, Melody Guy, and the staff at Ballantine Books for their superb editorial and design wisdom. She was able to see the shining potential in our initial rough ideas.

A great debt of thanks is owed to Adrienne Ingrum, a skilled organizer, meticulous editor, and a patient Christian woman, whose project management is largely responsible for assembling the professional personnel, as well as harvesting the vast array of recipes, text, and photographs.

To our project team: Sherry Bailey, who unwearyingly and carefully typed recipes and maintained numerous files; Roscoe Betsill, food stylist who made our food photogenic; Zana Bilue, who made the project come alive with her student recipe testers (Tah'swanna Khali Davis, Tiani Watso, John Gamble-Jennins, and Quiyona Gould) who prepared the recipes in the Abyssinian kitchen and presented tastings for the church staff; William Boyd, who provided the color photography; Tonya Hopkins, who began collecting the recipes; Adrienne Ingrum, who managed the project; and Booker Mattison, who interviewed key contributors and captured their stories of faith and food.

An abundance of thanks is extended to our pastor, Dr. Calvin O. Butts III, for his time, wisdom, encouragement, and willingness to venture into this bold new area of ministry.

To God be the glory for the great things He has done. Keep the faith!

Rev. Calvin O. Butts III

Contents

Breads 189

Desserts 209

A Word from Our Pastor, Reverend Dr. Calvin O. Butts III

Reverend Dr. Calvin Butts, pastor of The Abyssinian Baptist Church

I have often said that far too many black people are digging their graves with their own teeth. If the church is truly interested in the salvation of the whole person, then it should be teaching what is good for us to eat and what is not. As a black Baptist preacher this was a difficult adjustment for me to make because one of the staples of the black Baptist preacher's diet is fried chicken. But when I was stricken with cancer, for the first time in my life I took a serious look at what I was eating. In the church, we readily sacrifice our time, our talent, and our treasure, but the hardest thing for many of us to sacrifice is a diet of unhealthy food. It usually takes illness to shock us into eating right, and for some, not even sickness and doctor's orders can force us to make changes in our diet.

Looking back at my life, I can see that I was a prime candidate for cancer. I kept a busy schedule, and the only exercise I got was walking between my house, my car, and my several destinations. A typical work day ended around nine at night. Fried pork chops, macaroni and cheese, collard greens, and a couple of pieces of cornbread was a common late-night dinner. After washing the meal down with a glass of lemonade, I'd have a wedge of sweet potato pie for dessert. By this time it was ten-thirty. Too wired to go to sleep, my nightcap was the late-night news.

A colon cancer diagnosis forced me to examine my life. Questions that I had researched, lectured on, and preached about flooded my mind. What is death? What comes after death? But the most difficult question that tore at my heart was whether I had been living right. Anyone who has honestly answered that question has come up with a resounding no. The moment we answer in the affirmative we have achieved perfection and we no longer have need of a Savior. I found myself focusing on my mortality. It humbles you to discover that your life is transitory. You're just a pilgrim and a stranger passing through. Although I was more than half of one hundred, I wasn't ready to go. Then the words that I had preached at countless funerals came to mind: death is no respecter of age, wealth, or position. In the final analysis I realized that we tempt death when we're not good stewards of our bodies, and I was undeniably guilty of polluting my temple.

God is near to us whenever we call on him,[1] so before I could drink from the bitter cup of self-pity, He enabled me to see how blessed I was. I had a wife, family, church members, and friends who were more than willing to stand with me during the greatest trial of my life. I thought about the cross, and how there is always a blessing on the other side of tribulation. Jesus said, "Most assuredly, I say to you, unless a grain of wheat falls into the ground and dies, it remains alone; but if it dies, it produces much grain."[2] This is a major theme of Scripture: sacrifice. I determined that though cancer was compromising my own body, I would use this sickness for good.[3] I started to focus on ways to get the church community to recognize the importance of preventing disease through healthy eating so that others would not have to wrestle with this cancerous evil.

My eating habits have changed dramatically. When I get home from work I eat half a cantaloupe and drink eight ounces of water. Rarely do I eat dinner after seven, and fried food is no longer a part of my diet. I rise early to start my day with exercise, and instead of staying up to watch the late-night news I read a few passages of scripture before going to bed. Now some would argue, "Everything in moderation. You can have a pork chop or a piece of cornbread with butter from time to time." Yes you can, because God gave us a will that He will not override. But God is not mocked, whatsoever a man soweth, that shall he also reap.[4] So we owe it to ourselves to sow healthy foods into our temples. If we can take the scraps that were first given to us by the slave master and make those scraps taste so good that some church folk would fight the preacher before giving them up, we can certainly take foods that are truly good for us and make them taste even better. I'm a living witness, and many of the recipes in this book testify to that fact.

Some people don't know what it means to truly feel good. Since they were children they've been drinking and eating unhealthy foods loaded with preservatives. They've gained weight and never lost it, and although they've managed to function, they aren't living an abundant life. Once they come down to a weight that is appropriate for their height, body type, and bone structure, they're amazed.

This is similar to the experience that people have before they enter into a personal relationship with Jesus Christ. They may have been in church all their lives, but once they get hit by the Holy Spirit they start shouting and crying and tears begin to flow. They become consumed by a power that fills their temple and a complete lifestyle change is the result.

Eating right requires a lifestyle change. It takes prayer, discipline, meditation, and the study of God's Word. In his many parables on the kingdom of God, Jesus talked about the importance of pursuing what is valuable. These parables show that the kingdom of God is strikingly different from the world we live in. In the world you hate your enemies and love your friends. In the kingdom of God you're required to love your enemies.[5] In the world everyone is striving to be number one, but in the kingdom of God the last are first and the first are last.[6] That contradicts the way we naturally think, and so is abandoning foods that an overwhelming majority of people around you are eating. But Jesus instructs us to resist what is commonplace in the world. Yes, it is hard, but we're talking about saving lives. The church should take the lead in matters of physical salvation as well as spiritual salvation. So I'm issuing a challenge to churches across the country to prepare foods that will help us live longer—dishes that will keep our blood pressure from skyrocketing and keep our sugar levels stable. This will not only benefit us, it will benefit our children and grandchildren. They'll grow up and ask for steamed broccoli instead of collard greens with pig knuckles.

Endnotes:

1. Deuteronomy 4:7 (NLT)
2 John 12:24 (NKJV)
3 Genesis 50:20 (CEV)
4 Galatians 6:7 (KJV)
5 Matthew 5:44 (KJV)
6 Matthew 20:16 (KJV)

FOOD FOR THE SOUL

The Abyssinian Kitchen and Table

BOB GORE

food has been an important part of the Abyssinian Baptist Church since its founding in 1808. In the 1920s, when the church moved from downtown Manhattan to its current home in Harlem, women from the church served home-cooked meals to the men who cleared the land for construction. When the building was completed in 1923 it was the largest Protestant church in the world. Today food plays a significant part in many church events, but to understand the role food has played in the church, it is first necessary to understand the evolution of the food ministry at Abyssinian.

Six years after the church moved into its Harlem home, the stock market crashed, and the hardships that followed the nationwide economic collapse were magnified in neighborhoods like Harlem, which by the late 1920s had almost 200,000 people of African descent.

Reverend Dr. Adam Clayton Powell Sr. once said that when people are hungry they will pray. As the pastor who navigated Abyssinian through the rough waters of the Great Depression, it was undoubtedly those prayers that inspired him to meet the needs of the people. He gave his twenty-four-year-old son, Adam Clayton Powell Jr., a $1,000 gift to start a free food kitchen and together they started it in the church gymnasium. Area merchants donated food and church volunteers prepared meals for a thousand people a day.

Church member Virginia Morgan recalls that although the Depression was raging outside, "when you came in the church you wouldn't know it at all because the Spirit was there. Once you walked in you could feel it." Feisty, chatty, and still spry at ninety years young, Miss Virginia became a member of Abyssinian the same year the new building was erected, and unless the weather is bad you'll still find her at service every Sunday and at prayer meeting each Wednesday. Miss Virginia is the younger sister of the legendary Beatrice Talley, whom she still affectionately calls Miss Talley. Of all the great cooks who have passed through Abyssinian's kitchen, Beatrice Talley is the one for whom the church fellowship hall is named.

Of Miss Virginia's six sisters, four of them, including Virginia and Beatrice, migrated to Harlem from Macon, North Carolina, and became members of Abyssinian. Miss Virginia says that her whole family could cook because they were brought up to cook. She and her sisters learned by watching their mother, who baked the communion bread for the First Baptist Church in Macon from scratch. Miss Virginia's mother would take a yeast cake and soak it in a little milk and water. She got her flour ready by sprinkling it with a dash of salt. "Once the yeast cake was ready she would mix it with the flour in a big bowl with butter or oil—either one would do just fine. She'd get her hands clean—real clean. Then she'd get in that bowl, and beat it up. Beat it up into a nice ball, and roll it out real flat." She then took a cutter

The Powells, Proctor, and Food

Some of Adam Clayton Powell Sr.'s earliest memories involved food. When he was a young boy growing up in rural Virginia in the late 1800s, breakfast was served religiously at six a.m. "It usually consisted of fried pork, corn pone cooked in the skillet or ashes, and coffee made of rye. Once in a while we had white bread, and ham and molasses on Sunday morning. One year the crops were so poor that our corn and wheat were exhausted in April. We lived on dried apples and black-eyed peas for six weeks until the new crops were matured."[1] Even after Powell became an adult the smell of dried apples still made him queasy.

When Powell migrated north in the early 1900s, he took his love of food with him. Adam Clayton Powell Jr. recalled that life in their household on 134th Street between Seventh and Eighth Avenues was built on three things—breakfast, dinner, and prayer. "For breakfast we had a different hot bread every morning—muffins, biscuits, cornbread, loaves of hot oatmeal bread with handfuls of raisins and blueberries sprinkled through them; pancakes so big that they seemed to be a yard wide but, in fact, were only the size of a big frying pan because pancake griddles had not yet been invented" and Mrs. Powell churned plenty of butter to slather on that homemade bread. In those days it was unthinkable to bring anything already baked into your home. Dinner at the Powell household was as scrumptious as breakfast. Although Mrs. Powell prepared dinner with thrift, her selection was never dull. "A fifteen-pound leg of mutton on Sunday ended up on Friday or Saturday as lamb croquettes; during intervening days it appeared as ragout, stew, hash, and various and sundry other inventions."[2]

Dr. Proctor changes following an eleven a.m. service in 1996, one of the many times after his retirement that he served as guest preacher. With him is his son, Herbert Proctor, whose wife Patricia Leila Proctor's recipe for Baked Fillet of Sole with Cheese is on page 121.

Adam Clayton Powell Sr. was not just a fisher of men. He was also an avid fisher of the sea and had fished the world over. After New York's winter thaw you would find the elder Powell on the bank of some body of water and in the spring and summer the family would have his catch of the day three or four days a week. But dinner was not just limited to mutton and fish. Powell Jr. recalled that, "when the hucksters drove the blocks with barrels of rabbits we had Hassenpfeffer every day. Quarts of Lynnhaven oysters were sent to us from Virginia. Huge smoked country hams came from West Virginia, sometimes with little white worms crawling around in them, and then my father would say, 'It's in good shape.' Fresh greens were always cooked with this ham, from wild watercress in the spring to winter kale." Dinner also provided occasions for the younger Powell to develop his belief that the Bible was, in fact, inerrant. "My father was the only human being in the world, I am sure, who could take an ordinary duck, usually served in quarters, and carve it so that eight people would have more than enough to eat. I never doubted for once the miracle of Jesus feeding the five thousand when I saw the way my father could carve and feed our family and the unexpected guests who always dropped in."[3]

It was well known that Adam Clayton Powell Jr.'s successor, Dr. Samuel DeWitt Proctor, loved pork chops. If you prepared them just right and served them up with corn pudding, hot macaroni and cheese, and apple cobbler he would famously exclaim, "Great gobbles to wobbles!" Proctor's son Herb remembers that pork wasn't good for consumption when it first came in vogue. "That didn't bother my dad. His response was, 'the pig has brought me safe this far.'" However, Mr. Proctor also recalls that his father developed high blood pressure when he was in his forties. "He lived with it. He took medication for it. And he developed heart problems when he was fifty-eight. This prompted him to become health-conscious. He started to exercise. He believed in exercising as much as possible. He had an exercise cycle in his bedroom that he would ride every day. It wasn't anything that he balked at. He wanted to do it. He encouraged me and my brothers to be moderate in what we ate, and to exercise, to walk—do something. He cut back on the sweets and ate bananas for the potassium. He encouraged us because of the health problems that he developed. I would say too that the change and moderation in his diet helped him, it prolonged his life and made him healthier."

Reverend Butts was one of the hundreds of students that Dr. Proctor mentored. Dr. Proctor brought Reverend Butts to Abyssinian when he was still a student at Union Theological Seminary. Reverend Butts's commitment to using his sickness as a lightning rod to effect change in his congregation was undoubtedly influenced by Proctor's handling of his illness. Herb Proctor recounts that "he advised the congregation from the pulpit about good foods and how to do things in moderation. He wanted them to be healthy. He promoted walking as an exercise because he himself walked. He wanted people's blood pressure to be down, he wanted men to have their prostates screened, and he wanted women to have their annual checkups. He emphasized preventive care. Get your checkup. Stick to what the doctor is saying. If you have a condition, pay attention to what you're supposed to do so the condition stays in check."

In later years Dr. Proctor preferred his pork chops baked, not fried, and he didn't eat as much of the apple cobblers. Herb Proctor does mention with a grin, however, that "every now and then he would sneak and get some of his favorite foods."

1. Powell, Adam Clayton. *Against the Tide: An Autobiography.* New York: Richard R. Smith, 1938.
2. Powell, Adam Clayton Jr. *Adam by Adam: The Autobiography of Adam Clayton Powell Jr.* New York: Kensington Publishing Corp., 1971.
3. Ibid.

and delicately sectioned the dough into tiny squares, marking each one with a cross. Because she didn't cut the dough all the way through, after it was baked it could be broken up easily and given to the people during the communion service. Beatrice Talley brought this homespun recipe to Harlem and used it to make her rolls in the Abyssinian kitchen. The only difference was that she would let the dough rise so that her rolls would turn out both fluffy and delicious.

Reverend Powell Sr. approached Beatrice Talley about taking over the Abyssinian kitchen. Miss Virginia's eyes light up when she recalls that Reverend Powell wasn't the only person who recognized that her sister knew her way around a kitchen. "Everybody knew she could cook. No questions asked. And whenever she cooked it wouldn't be too long before all the food was gone." Miss Virginia describes a typical Sunday: "We'd get to the church at six a.m. and have breakfast ready by seven or seven-thirty. Miss Talley cooked, and I served. I would run around and get the dining room all fixed up. I love flowers, so every table had lots of flowers. I would set the tablecloths while Miss Talley baked the bread. People came in special to have breakfast, but they mostly liked her hot rolls with coffee. Reverend Powell and his family used to live in an apartment upstairs above the church, so we'd send his food up on a tray. He would come down mostly for dinner after church. After service he'd stand at the door of the Fellowship Hall and greet the people. Everybody loved talking to him, you know, he's the pastor. Friendliness was one of his better qualities, so he wouldn't shoo you off. One thing about him, he made everybody feel welcome. That was the good part. Everybody was like family."

The dinner menu seldom changed, but each week Miss Talley would have choices: "Pretty brown fried chicken,

Beatrice Talley.

deep fat to fry it because that makes a big difference. Nice baked ham, some good string beans or greens, potato salad or baked potato." A weekly staple was tossed salad made of crisp iceberg lettuce, garden fresh tomatoes, and thinly sliced cucumbers. "Miss Talley left the skin on the cucumbers to give the salad a little color, and she made her own dressing out of mayonnaise, white vinegar, and oil." Dessert was usually an apple or peach cobbler baked from scratch.

"One thing about cooking, you have to study the people to see what they like. People like chicken, and they like string beans. But they really liked those beans the way Miss Talley cooked them. First she would boil a ham for half an hour with onions, green peppers, and whole garlic cloves to bring out the flavor. After she put that ham in the oven to brown she would soak the beans in the juice. That's what made them taste so good. Then she'd take that ham and carve it into beautiful slices. Sometimes instead of having taters she'd have macaroni and cheese. She'd use spaghetti noodles instead of elbow noodles to make it a little bit different." Miss Virginia smiles slyly before continuing. "I had my own tricks, but I'm not going to share them with you."

This was before the days of ranges and refrigerators. "We loved to cook so much, and we kept that kitchen clean because we had to get around it. We had a wood and coal burning stove and an icebox. I remember that meal tickets were fifty cents for breakfast, and dinner was a dollar and a half. If you wanted to take your food out it was a little bit more because we had to give you a paper plate. Once you got your ticket, you could either stand at the door to the kitchen to be served for takeout, or sit down if you wanted me to wait on you. I would give you water and a napkin and ask you what you wanted. We usually had a special table set up for those who finished eating and just wanted to sit there and talk. It's good for the older people because if they don't have meals at the church, what they got to do but sit up in the house? Instead they can come here, meet the family, and talk."

Beatrice Talley never gave too much thought to when she would retire. One Wednesday night at prayer meeting she raised her hands in the service "like she knew she was going to pass away from here." Miss Virginia still gets misty-eyed when she remembers that fateful night. Miss Talley never made it back to the kitchen. It was certainly the end of an era. But just as Moses handed the mantle of leadership over to someone whom God had been preparing for the task, after Beatrice Talley's passing Deacon Allen Mintz was already writing another page in the history of the Abyssinian kitchen.

C. Vernon Mason fondly remembers that Deacon Mintz was "famous for the aroma of the bread he baked on Sunday mornings. Sometimes it would be difficult to concentrate on what was going on in the service because that aroma would be coming up from the kitchen." Mason, who proudly donned an apron and volunteered as a food server in the kitchen, was a high-profile attorney who worked on several cases that garnered national attention. "One of the wonderful things about Abyssinian is that when you're at the church, your job is not important. You'll have ushers who are CEOs of their companies and choir members who are partners in law firms. Part of what we got from the leadership and preaching of [former pastor] Dr. Samuel DeWitt Proctor, and Dr. Butts, and the elders and other leaders in the church was that it really didn't matter what our careers were because everyone is called to serve. The joy of wearing an apron and working in the kitchen was not just practicing the lessons we were taught, but in helping new members see what service meant."

"Fellowship and food have always been synonymous here at Abyssinian. This tradition has been in place since 1808. We don't call the place where the food is served the Fellowship Hall for nothing. Deacon Mintz embodied this tradition. You couldn't find a better baker, and his rolls were superior to any you could buy from a bakery. But he was a very quiet, humble person. He was just absolutely incredible. Highly regarded, and well respected. People loved him. I had the privilege of serving with him in the kitchen and on the deacon board. When I talk about Deacon Mintz's rolls, the food is just one part of it. What I think people had such tremendous respect for is that over those years this brother came in, went out, and bought all of those ingredients, and did it voluntarily. What was lifted up was the service, and the food that he cooked was the result of that service. As delicious as those rolls were, they were a symbol of his love for his church family. His ministry was within his service, and it was that way with all of us. It may be while you're in the Fellowship Hall serving, or having food that you're providing a listening ear to somebody who needs to talk. You don't have to fix the problem. You may not even have a solution, but you might be the only person who listened to them all week. Our time in the Fellowship Hall was never limited to just the consumption of food. You were

Deacon Allen Mintz, 1998. For decades Mintz oversaw the church kitchen. Along with his reputation for tireless work, he was known for his mouthwatering dinner rolls.

taught a number of lessons; you could counsel or be counseled. You might see somebody you hadn't seen in a number of years, or renew an old acquaintance. And then you had visitors and new members who were meeting people from Abyssinian for the first time. Certainly we ate Deacon Mintz's cooking because our bodies needed nourishing, but we had something else that needed nourishing too—our spirits. That's what I associate with the food fellowship that goes on in the Abyssinian kitchen."

Martha Hatcher already had a reputation as a great cook before she joined Abyssinian. In addition to working as a dietitian for the New York City Board of Education for twenty-five years, she ran a catering business that serviced an upscale downtown clientele for two decades

As a prominent attorney, Reverend Mason earned a national reputation by representing high-profile civil rights cases. Mid-career, he was called to the ministry.

and was a caterer for Bon Apetit's grand opening in the early '70s. "Even though my husband was a member of Abyssinian, I didn't start coming here until he was ordained a deacon in 1978. Mr. Mintz was in charge of the kitchen at that time, and little by little I melted into the pot. After Deacon Mintz passed in 1996 I took over."

Sunday breakfast and dinner were not the only meals that were prepared in the Abyssinian kitchen. There were events such as the Ida Belle Newman Luncheon for members over seventy, the Deacons, Deaconesses, Trustees Sermon, and the Annual Women's Day Celebration, which included a fish fry on Friday and brunch on Saturday.

While Mrs. Hatcher was running the Abyssinian kitchen, the *New York Times* sought her out when they did their cookbook. The *Times* included her recipe for string beans, even though, Hatcher says, "they didn't get it right. They said you cook the beans for three or four hours, but you only need to cook them for fifteen or twenty minutes. If you cooked them for three or four hours they'd be pureed."

BOB CORE

Hatcher's attention to detail is one reason why her food has always stood out. "See, I'm very, very particular about the way I want things done. I cook most foods the way I like to have them taste if I'm eating. When people know that I'm cooking they will say that Martha is cooking, or Mrs. Hatcher is cooking, so it's going to be good. I guess it's the method and the seasonings that I use that will make it a little bit different from someone else. And the way you set up your food and display it on your serving dishes is important too. Time management has an awful lot

Deaconess Martha Hatcher at a Celebration of the Deaconess Board, 1982.

to do with it because you want the food cooked at the right time so that it doesn't over-set. When you pace your cooking with the order of the event, then a dish that's supposed to be served cold will be cold, and something that's supposed to be hot will be hot.

"I always used fresh ingredients. You could buy peeled potatoes or peeled carrots, but I would peel them myself. I would make three or four hundred muffins a week. The cornbread, all the cakes and pies, everything I did from scratch. To give you an example of how particular I am, most

Reverend Butts serving Fannie Pennington, whose recipe for North Carolina–Style Ham Hocks is on page 74, and Jonnetta Cole during an annual Women's Day celebration.

people don't take the bone out when they make salmon croquettes. They leave the black skin on the meat. I clean the salmon completely when it comes out of the can. I remember when I made salmon croquettes for a Women's Day breakfast, and Congressman Charles Rangel came. He said that those were the best salmon croquettes that he'd ever tasted, and he took some home to his wife. So it's little things like that, the compliments you get, that serve as your feedback. Then you know that you've made a difference to someone else's palate."

Other luminaries who had the pleasure of feasting on Martha Hatcher's delicacies when they visited Abyssinian were singer

A snapshot from Dr. Proctor's retirement luncheon, 1989. Left to right: Deacon James Hatcher, Deaconess Martha Hatcher, and Dr. Samuel DeWitt Proctor.

Leontyne Price, musician Wynton Marsalis, and Zubin Mehta of the New York Philharmonic Orchestra. Hatcher prepared the food for the installation service for Reverend Butts when he took over as senior pastor after Dr. Proctor's retirement in 1989. She used her forty-five years of food service experience to upgrade the kitchen at Abyssinian into the commercial-grade facility that it is today.

Mrs. Hatcher ran the kitchen off and on for eleven years, until the mid 1990s. During that time she hired Miss Myrna, who eventually took over after Deacon Wattell Hines and Deacon Ben Barrow, owner of Harlem's Pan Pan Restaurant, had a stint at the helm.

Miss Myrna's high-energy working style defies her years. "I don't feel my age, to tell you the truth. I have to remember it sometimes, I honestly do, until they tease me down in the kitchen saying, 'Miss Myrna, you have to remember you're sixty-five, you're getting up in age.' My response is, 'Yes I am,' and they say, 'You move around better than we do,' because I've always moved very fast. That's the way I am.

"Abyssinian, I just fell in love with it. It started out as a part-time job;

Deacon Benjamin Barrow, far left, of Pan Pan Restaurant, with volunteer Eugene Zambori and future head of the Abyssinian kitchen Myrna Sanders.

however, it's no longer part-time. I used to work only Friday, Saturday, and Sunday, but now a lot of times I'm working forty-five or fifty-five hours a week. Last week, for example, the Brotherhood (a male ministry engaged in prayer and study to support the pastor and other church activities) had an event for two hundred people on Friday night. They requested pasta and chicken wings, cake and punch. The very next morning the Male Chorus had their annual luncheon and 250 people attended. They had a full meal—half a baked chicken, stuffing, string beans, rolls, and a fresh fruit salad and peach cobbler for dessert. We were back in here at five o'clock on Sunday morning because breakfast starts at eight, and we usually serve about one hundred fifty people. Breakfast is supposed to go no later than a quarter of twelve, but if service runs over, then we run over also. Dinner starts shortly after the morning service, but people are lined up before the service is over. We serve about one hundred twenty-five people for dinner. I do work very hard and I expect people to work hard like I do, so you'll very seldom see me sitting down. Today I've already made

"Miss Myrna" Sanders—out of the kitchen—in the sanctuary.

Women's Day Celebration 1990. Seated, bottom row, left to right: Cheryl Washington, Eloise Mills, Chairwoman Shirley V. Corbino, Speaker for the Day Reverend Sharon Williams, Co-chairwoman Deaconess Jackie Jones. Standing, top row, left to right: Fannie Pennington, Deaconess Martha Hatcher, Trustee LaVergne Trawick, Pauline Grant, Reverend Dr. Calvin Butts III, Mrs. Patricia Butts, Deaconess Barbara Hines, Church Clerk Venia R. Davis, Naomi Green, and Judge Donna Mills.

BOB GORE

Eugene Zambori, food service volunteer, in the Abyssinian kitchen.

ten peach pies, twelve blueberry pies, and ten apple pies. And I still have to make sweet potato."

Like many African Americans, the cooks in the Abyssinian kitchen have adhered to the tradition of preparing sumptuous meals with pork. But under Miss Myrna's watch, beef or pork is seldom used because the eating habits of the congregants have evolved.

"When I first came here we were cooking the vegetables with bacon. But a lot of people complained that they didn't eat that anymore. So I figured that rather than having to keep explaining why we cooked with pork we would just stop. Now we use smoked turkey in the greens. For those who don't eat any type of meat we offer a tossed salad made with romaine lettuce. In general, we're doing more vegetables. This Sunday we're going to have a vegetable medley of broccoli, cauliflower, and carrots. Instead of butter I'll use a little margarine, chicken base, and basil. Then I'll steam it and drop in strips of red pepper at the last minute. There are still occasions when we'll do either smothered pork chops or stuffed pork chops with an apple stuffing. Interestingly though, there's not a drop-off in the number we serve when we cook pork, especially if we do barbecued ribs."

High fat and cholesterol are not the only things that have been modified in some of the meals that are served in the Abyssinian kitchen. The problem of high sodium has also been addressed. "We are using a lot less salt, even though a few will say that the food is a little bland sometimes. But we figured that if people want more salt they can put it on themselves."

Although Miss Myrna tries to make the meals that she prepares healthier, she affectionately calls the recipe that the congregation most often requests cholesterol bread. "When I make my broccoli cheese cornbread, everybody wants to eat. I came across that recipe years ago in some old recipes that my mother gave me that were written on pages that had turned yellow. (See the recipe on page 199.) I call it cholesterol bread because there is a lot of cholesterol in it. But the people really do love it."

Miss Myrna will be sixty-six in July, and thoughts of retirement have become a constant companion. Nevertheless, she still solicits God's help to make it through each day. "Before I come in I get on my knees and pray, 'God please help me to do my best,' and that's all I can do."

The wonderful meals prepared in the kitchen and the fellowship that has sprung up around them have been among Abyssinian's best blessings. The Beatrice Talley Fellowship Hall has been an enduring symbol of the food and the fellowship that has had such a lasting impact on the church's nearly two-hundred-year history.

Zana Billue and students at work recipe testing.

ABYSSINIAN BAPTIST CHURCH
MEN'S DAY
50TH ANNIVERSARY
COOKING FOR CHRIST

Cooking for a New Day:
The Health Ministry at Abyssinian

The epidemic of heart disease, diabetes, stroke, and cancer is causing tremendous concern in the African American community, and the black church is not immune. These maladies hamper the work of the gospel because a strong body is crucial to a healthy spiritual life. This is our reasonable service to our Maker. The pastors of Abyssinian Baptist Church, from Thomas Paul to such spiritual giants as Adam Clayton Powell Sr., congressman and civil rights leader Adam Clayton Powell Jr., and educator Dr. Samuel DeWitt Proctor, have been written about extensively for their groundbreaking leadership. History will prove that the visionary leadership of Reverend Dr. Calvin Butts, while addressing many important social issues of our day, was revolutionary in the matter of food. His boldness in teaching the church community to rethink the way we select, prepare, and consume foods is blazing new trails and leading the way to greater community wellness.

According to statistics compiled by the American Heart Association, "cardiovascular diseases rank as the number one killer of African Americans, claiming the lives of 37 percent of African Americans who die each year. Cancer follows cardiovascular disease, killing almost 22 percent. About 4 in every 10 black adults have cardiovascular disease. This includes diseases of the heart, stroke, high blood pressure, congestive heart failure, congenital cardiovascular defects, hardening of the arteries, and other diseases of the circulatory system. The rate of high blood pressure in blacks in the United States is among the highest in the world. Compared with whites, blacks are much more likely to have high blood pressure, less likely to engage in physical activity, more likely to be overweight or obese, and more likely to have diabetes. All these factors raise their cardiovascular disease risk."[1]

The statistics for cancer are equally sobering. The American Cancer Society reports that African Americans have the highest death rate in every form of cancer among all ethnic groups in the United States. Cancers related to nutrition, physical inactivity, and obesity are preventable.[2] We ignore these statistics at our own peril, and though God is a healer and He is merciful, when we request healing and continue to live irresponsibly we ask God to go against His law of sowing and reaping. God's people perish because of lack of knowledge.[3] Since 2002 the Health Ministry at Abyssinian has been on a mission to ensure that this knowledge is made available to all who would listen.

There is debate and discussion about the quality of the health care that we receive in the African American community, but there is no debate about our ability to prevent or control some medical conditions through proper nutrition. We know that heart disease, diabetes, and some cancers can be prevented if we follow healthy nutritional guidelines. The Abyssinian Health Ministry has been instrumental in raising awareness about what we can do nutritionally to prevent some of these chronic, debilitating, and life-threatening diseases.

One of the health concerns that led to the official formation of the Abyssinian Health Ministry was weight management. It quickly developed into a ministry that was not only concerned with the health of the physical body, but also the condition of the mind and the spirit. The ministry chairperson, Mrs. Patricia Butts, recalls that when a group of about 30 women came together to discuss the difficulty of weight loss, it quickly became evident that, for many, the excess weight they carried was a symptom of emotional and mental stress. "Each time we gathered together we found that there were a lot of other issues that were of concern, and most of them were exaggerated by obesity. We started to address these issues, and not just here at Abyssinian, because these were problems that affect the entire community. For example, too often we handled stress by overindulging in comfort foods, the rich, calorie-laden foods we ate as children—macaroni and cheese, desserts, or homemade bread. Now we eat these foods along with fatty, sugary, salty fast foods.

"Food also plays a central role in our celebrations; when we rejoice and when we mourn, we usually eat. Despite very busy schedules, when we come together for holidays, family gatherings, and funerals, we find the time to make that special dish, that great calorie-rich potato salad, candied yams laden with butter and sugar, or a pot of greens cooked with ham hocks or fat back. Couple this kind of eating pattern with lack of exercise and the pounds begin to creep up.

"We have found that we would be a lot better off if we added more fruits and vegetables to our diets. We would also benefit if we stopped overcooking the vegetables that we do eat until all of the nutrients are depleted. Historically when our relatives cooked vegetables until they were soft they would drink the pot liquor or soak it up with cornbread. We no longer do that so we lose the benefits of the nutrient-dense liquid."

The Health Ministry conducts seminars that feature doctors and nutritionists who discuss topics ranging from portion size and calorie awareness to heart disease, diabetes, and cancer to mental health, weight management, and nutrition. The ministry also provides information on the impact foods have on the body, nutrients lost or altered in the preparation of foods, and food-growing methods; has allowed members and friends to taste nutrient-dense foods that have been prepared in a way that preserves the nutritional value; and also offers the opportunity to lose weight together through a structured program, and through a friendly weight-loss competition between our church and other churches in our community.

The Abyssinian Health Ministry also recognizes the connection between mind, body, and spirit and also conducts sessions on prayer and meditation, and weekly exercise classes that are free and open to the public. It is obvious why we focus on prayer, and we include meditation as the practice of learning to quiet our minds and hearts to enable us to focus on what God has to say to us. Meditation is also taught in the Health Ministry as a form of quieting the physical body in order to better manage our stress levels.

Because balance is the key to life, the Health Ministry doesn't just emphasize what people need to cut. For the Lenten season, our encouragement to the church was not to focus so much on what you were going to take away, but to focus on ways of shoring up your spiritual life because getting started on the road to better health is about surrendering. We encouraged those who no longer have the traditional family meal where everybody comes to the table to have healthy meals together. We also asked them to commit to mind new scriptures. People usually have their favorite scripture and they can recite it from memory. Our challenge was for them to go back and revisit the Book, and perhaps learn some new scriptures.

Eating and enjoying food is not sinful. The sin is not in the eating but in overeating and knowingly eating unhealthy foods. Acknowledging the time constraints that most of us face in everyday living, the Abyssinian Health Ministry encourages taking at least two easy steps toward wellness: simply including more fruits, vegetables, and whole grains in the daily diet, and adding some form of exercise that you can stick with, like walking. It is also important to include a healthy *variety* of fruits, vegetables, and whole grains.

Take a positive approach to wellness and look at what you can add to your lifestyle to make a positive difference, not at what you might feel is deprivation by taking your favorite foods away. When you do eat your high-calorie comfort foods, or participate fully in the eating celebrations, do so in moderation and pay attention to actual serving sizes.

We encourage a look back at the positive tradition of our families gathering together around the breakfast or dinner table. Even in today's busy world, take time to slow down and be with your family, take time to prepare a healthy meal, take time to take care of yourself. When it comes to health, the old adages still ring true, *we are what we eat,* and if we continue to eat in what we know to be unhealthy ways, *we are literally digging our graves with our teeth.* Physicians who have come to the health ministry tell us that if we led healthier lifestyles they would write fewer prescriptions. The tendency is for a doctor to prescribe one medication and then prescribe another to offset the side effects that you experienced from the first.

The Health Ministry has discovered that what most people need after they receive information is encouragement. Mrs. Butts explains that "we are in the midst of a weight-loss challenge with another church and we have a large group of people who joined our church to be in this competition. Some members are doing extremely well, but others who have gotten off to a slow start will say, 'I need more support.' It takes a lot of work and discipline, and you've got to be willing to put in the work. You can't join a group and think that just going and having conversations is going to do it. You've got to make a decision about what it is you need to cut out of your diet and ways that you can be more active. I think we're not always realistic about that. Ultimately, though, the success is in the fact that people are thinking about their health, and they're thinking about what they're eating. The American Cancer Society and the American Diabetes Association are supplying prizes for 'the winning losers'—those who lose the most weight win."

In response to the dramatic increase in the number of children being diagnosed with diabetes, a physician who is a member of the church conducted a seminar on childhood obesity. Mrs. Butts maintains that "this problem is not just the fault of the children. When I was coming up through school, physical education was a regularly scheduled class that you had to attend, usually more than once a week. But funding for physical education programs and even team sports has been cut in a lot of cities because of budget deficits. We may not have been eating the best when I was young, but we were burning up more calories than kids today. I don't think I knew anyone who had diabetes. We also had things like the Presidential Fitness Test, where we had to meet minimum requirements for sit-ups, jumping jacks, climbing rope, and other exercises. Those types of incentives encouraged us to be active. Someone was at home to cook for us when we got home from school. Whether it was a grandmother or an aunt, there was someone there and they would prepare a home-cooked meal. Now it's fast food and frozen dinners for the kids. I understand that for working parents it's difficult to come in at eight o'clock at night, check homework, make sure things are set up for the next day, and also think about a complete nutritious meal. But it has to become a priority." Changing the palate of tradition and habit will take time, but the Abyssinian Health Ministry will continue to be diligent about serving up healthy information that will allow us to better manage our health and to respect our bodies and treat them as the temples that house our souls. A healthy spirit, body, and mind is necessary to do the work our faith commands us to do.

A Health Advocate

Dr. Anita Underwood has been a member of Abyssinian for the past seventeen years. She is an Organizational Psychologist by profession, but her passion has been researching, selecting, and preparing healthier foods since graduate school. "If I was not a psychologist, I would probably be a nutritionist or a health guru. Over the years, I have read many books from different perspectives on health; including those from traditional medical professionals, nutritionists, and alternative health practitioners. What I have discovered is that there are common elements that exist across the board. For example, we should avoid white sugar, white flour, and salt. The other common points are avoiding fried foods and preservatives. To keep our bodies hydrated, we should drink lots of water, and distilled water probably has the least amount of chemicals. Some experts have said we should drink half of our body weight in water."

Underwood first heard about the importance of a healthy diet when she was in the sixth grade. "My mother worked for a cancer research and treatment hospital and shared information with me about the relationship between stress, food, and health. On occasions when I complained about an ache or not feeling well, she would say, 'sounds like you need more water, or more calcium, or add this nutrient to your diet.' When I was a child, I watched as older people got sick and heard doctors tell them to get rid of the salt in their diets and to cut down on the fatty meat. I would say to my mother, 'If they tell you to get rid of that food item later in life, it must be bad for you early on, so why eat it to begin with?' "

Underwood has been a vegetarian since 1975 and the knowledge that she has accumulated over the years she readily shares. "The Bible talks about grains, fruits, and vegetables being our meat,[4] so from my point of view that's more natural than eating processed and chemically induced foods. God has given us these natural foods, and yet people choose to eat things that are harmful to them. So we have the choice to eat the apple or the potato chips with the trans fats. Can any of us who are vegetarians get sick? Sure, vegetarianism is not fool proof to perfect health. But my philosophy has been to be eat as healthly as you can. A nutritionist I have used over the years, suggested some guidelines to assist me in avoiding unhealthy snacks; "Do not have anything that has over thirteen grams per serving of sugar or do not buy anything that has over two grams of fat." This gives people a measurement that they can keep in mind when they shop. He also suggested that anything that comes in a wrapper or a bag that you have to rip open to eat is probably processed and has chemicals in it. If you read the label and you see a lot of words that you can't pronounce, those are the additives that you want to stay away from.

"People should look for whole foods, which are fresh vegetables and fruits that are grown naturally in the ground or on a vine. These foods are not engineered and add fiber to your diet. For those who do eat meat, they should buy organic or free-range meats because those animals are fed whole and natural foods, rather than growth hormones."

Over the years Dr. Underwood has amassed a considerable cookbook collection that features vegetarian recipes that the garden variety carnivore may not be familiar with. "When you don't eat meat you don't have to feel like you're in withdrawal or deprived. I am always thinking about flavor and taste, therefore I have vegetarian Chinese, Mexican, and Caribbean cookbooks. I like going to ethnic grocery stores to purchase the diverse kinds of vegetables to cook creatively and fuse ethnic flavors. One of my favorite Italian recipes is eggplant parmesan. I will take eggplant and bread it with spelt bread crumbs and lightly sauté it in a little olive oil. When I make the tomato sauce I include freshly chopped garlic, and fresh onions, and then I add cayenne so it's good and spicy. I season it as though I'm making a meat sauce to ensure that there's plenty of flavor. Then I melt soy cheese over it. As a side dish I might steam some broccoli and then let it marinate in a dressing of olive oil and a little apple cider vinegar.

"If I'm cooking on the grill I might have a veggie burger with barbeque sauce. Tofu I only use on occasion. Before I grill that I'll marinate it in balsamic vinegar, olive oil, pepper sauce, and cilantro. Basically, there's a vegetarian alternative for everything. The drawback is that because you're using fresh ingredients you do more chopping, so the prep time may increase, but the cooking time decreases because you're not using meat."

Our Prayer

We know that the Almighty wants to give long life to those who love and serve God,[5] and to allow as much time as possible to those who don't so that they can make that all-important connection to God.[6] This book was designed with that in mind. We hope that our testimonies will inspire you to take a second look at healthy eating and to give thought to all that you eat so that your spirit can spend the rest of its days in a glorious, healthy temple!

Endnotes:

1 American Heart Association, "Heart Facts 2004: African Americans," www.americanheart.org, accessed June 26, 2004.

2 American Cancer Society, "Cancer Facts & Figures 2004," www.cancer.org/statistics, accessed June 26, 2004.

3 Hosea 4:6 (KJV)

4 Genesis 1:29-30 (NKJV)

5 Isaiah 46:4 (KJV)

6 2 Peter 3:4 (KJV)

Senior Choir
12:00 Noon   Beauitful Savior
Young People's Choir

OFFERING
THE SUPER
  (a)   HYMN #103 Leaning On The Ever
  (b)   NEW MEMBERS
  (c)   WITNESSING
  (d)   CONSECRATION
  (e)   THE BREAD
  (f)   THE CUP
  (g)   HYMN OF INSPIRATION
        #135   The Old Rugged Cross

BENEDICTION AND SEVEN FOLD AMEN
COMMITMENT

7:00 P.M. EVENING VESPERS

CALL TO WORSHIP   Congreg
HYMN   Mrs. Ef
INVOCATION
RESPONSIVE READING
SELECTION
INTRODUCTION OF
SPEAKERS

OFFERTORY
ANNOUNCEMENTS
HYMN
BENEDICTION

Ingredients:
_ red pepper, diced
_ green pepper, diced
One 1-ounce envelope onion soup
_ small onion, diced
3 carrots, sliced
One 28-ounce can crushed or puréed tomatoes
_ pound cabbage, cut into small pieces
4 stalks celery, diced
_ teaspoon pepper
_ teaspoon salt, optional
One 10-ounce package frozen mixed vegetables

Place red pepper, green pepper, onion, celery,
and carrots in a large saucepan. Add tomatoes.
Add onion soup mix, pepper, salt if using and 1
cup water. Cook for 30 minutes. Add cabbage.
Cook 20 minutes longer. Add frozen vegetables.
Continue cooking until vegetables are heated,
about 10 minutes.

Serves 6 to 8

Ingredients:
2 pounds pota
2-inch- thick

2 quarts chick
2 tablespoons
2 garlic clove
1 teaspoon sa
easpoon bla
orizo saus
ound fresh
pped in lar

k potatoes.

il fork tend
and lightly
n
atoes to pot

kale. Cook
is done, ab
whole s
age to soup.

utes. Remove
h-thick piec
p.

HE SONS OF ABYSSINIAN BAPTIST CHURCH
HE PASTOR .... Dr. A
USIC " A MIGHTY FORTRESS IS OUR GOD" ....D
MARKS ....
THE END

—o—

THE SESQUICENTENNIAL BANQUE
served by
THE PARENT-TEACHERS ASSOCATION OF THE
ABYSSINIAN BAPTIST CHURCH
Laura B. Thomas, Chairman
THURSDAY, MAY 21, 1959 at 7: P. M.

MENU

SESQUICENTENNIAL COCKTAIL, JUICE and SNACKS
ROAST VERMONT TURKEY with DRESSING
CRANBERRY SAUCE
BOUQUET OF BUTTERED FRESH VEGETABLES
COLE SLAW
SESQUICENTENNIAL YAM SOUFFLE'
MINIATURE BREAD
SESQUICENTENNIAL CAKE
CREME GLACE'
COOKIES
COFFEE
MINTS
CIGARETTES
BREAD - - Courtesy - SILVER CUP
CAKE - - Courtesy - BETTER CRUST COMPANY
Dual Filter Tarrytone - Courtesy - AMERICAN TOBACCO COMPANY
Matches - Courtesy - H. I. ZIMMERMAN

Solomon P. Weinberg
"Serving your every Insurance need"
604 Grand Concourse
New York 51, N. Y. — — Phone WY 3-3131

The Abyssinian Baptist Church

Women's and Men's Day Committees
Present
the 19th Annual Black College and Career Fair

Academic Excellence...

What Does a Good Education Mean to You?

Saturday, April 16, 2005
10:00 a.m. until 3:00 p.m.
Free Registration begins at 9:15 a.m.

The Abyssinian Baptist Church
132 Odell Clark Place (Formerly West 138th Street)

Free Hot Lunch Served
Morning Workshops and Panel Discussions
Book Scholarship Drawing to 3 Lucky Attendees

Meet Representatives from:
Several Historically Black Colleges and Universities
State Universities (S.U.N.Y.) and City Universities (C.U.N.Y.)
The College Board
Stanley Kaplan Preparatory and much more

Rev. Calvin O. Butts, III, Pastor
The Abyssinian Baptist Chruch
132 Odell Clark Place
212.862.7474

THE
RECIPES

HANSEN
VERNA
PHOTO
N.Y. N.Y.

Appetizers

Clockwise from bottom left: Cold Salmon Rosettes
with Caper Butter (page 40), Rumaki
(Water Chestnuts Wrapped in Bacon) (page 42),
and Tuna Monte Cristos (page 43).

Hot Crab Dip

Recipe from the kitchen of Felicia Gray, age 12

My extended family, the Jordans, have a holiday party every year to which they invite everyone to hang out and have a good time. The aroma of generations of recipes wafting from the kitchen tempt me when I enter their home. I don't eat before I go to the party, so I am usually starving by the time I get to my aunt Carolyn's house, and my first words are, "Where's the hot crab dip?" This tasty, creamy dip, served with some crusty bread, is great even if you're not a seafood lover!

Many crab dip recipes call for imitation crabmeat, but there's no place for "krab" here. Only real lump crabmeat makes it taste best. Serve it while it's hot with crackers, bite-size pieces of bread, or veggie sticks. It can also be presented in a bread bowl and served with a tray of fresh broccoli, carrots, zucchini, or crackers.

One 4-ounce package cream cheese, softened
$^1/_2$ cup mayonnaise
$^1/_4$ cup finely chopped onion
1 tablespoon fresh lemon juice
$^1/_2$ teaspoon hot pepper sauce
$^1/_2$ teaspoon Old Bay seasoning or other seasoned salt
6 ounces fresh or canned lump crabmeat, drained

Preheat the oven to 350°F.

Place all the ingredients except the crab in a medium bowl and blend together with a spatula. Stir in the crab. Turn the dip into a 1-quart casserole and bake, uncovered, for 30 minutes, or until heated through.

Makes 1 $^1/_3$ cups

Crab Cakes

Recipe from the kitchen of the Student Recipe Testers

The students kept asking if they could fix crab cakes for their family meal while they were testing recipes. We made these on the last day of testing, and they were quickly devoured as soon as they left the frying pan. We used a combination of lump and special crabmeats to minimize the cost.

One 8-ounce container lump crabmeat

One 8-ounce container backfin crabmeat

1 large shallot, finely chopped

1 tablespoon mayonnaise

1 tablespoon sour cream

2 teaspoons Worcestershire sauce

1 teaspoon Old Bay seasoning

2 teaspoons fresh lemon juice

1 large egg, beaten

2 cups panko (Japanese breadcrumbs)

$^1/_4$ cup vegetable oil, or as needed

Combine both types of crabmeat in a medium bowl; don't break up all the lumps. Add the shallot, mayonnaise, sour cream, Worcestershire sauce, Old Bay, and lemon juice and mix until well combined. Add the egg and mix again. Form the crabmeat mixture into cakes 2 inches wide and $^1/_4$ inch thick. Place the panko in a shallow bowl and coat the crab cakes with the panko. Heat the oil in a large skillet over medium-high heat. Add some of the crab cakes and fry until golden brown, 4 to 5 minutes each side. Remove from the skillet and drain on paper towels. Add more oil as needed and continue to fry the crab cakes until all the batter has been used.

Makes 8 to 10 crab cakes

Finger Sandwiches from a Brioche

Recipe from the kitchen of Mrs. Martha Hatcher

Mrs. Hatcher, a professional caterer who was in charge of the Abyssinian kitchen from the mid 1980s until the mid 1990s, comments, "I really enjoy using what I've learned working in food service to help the church. I'm seventy-two years old, but if I wasn't sick I would probably still have my catering business. I got hurt in 1978, but in spite of the two operations, if someone wants me to prepare something I tell them to let me know. Even though I can't do as much as I used to, I still do a little cooking because I still love cooking.

"Sometimes I would make a large brioche for my finger sandwiches. Brioche is a huge round loaf of bread with, of course, a flat bottom. Brioche can be ordered from a good specialty bakery and found at finer grocery stores. This recipe uses the center portion of the brioche—the white bread—to make finger sandwiches and allows the crust to retain its beautiful shape and serve as the container for the finger sandwiches. You've probably seen the watermelon rind used as a container for a melon salad. This

BILL BOYD

is the same principle. The cutting instructions in this recipe explain how to cut out the soft center bread for use in making sandwiches, leaving the crust in its original shape. The finished recipe looks like a big round loaf of bread with a radish rose on top. The radish rose is the 'handle' and when lifted off, it removes the top crust of the loaf and reveals the lovely finger sandwiches inside. I remember the first time I made a brioche for an event sponsored by the deaconess board. It was the funniest thing. While I was getting everything ready somebody said, 'Don't nobody want those old sandwiches?' So I think I must've made twelve, one for each table. When the event was over, everybody was just so happy. They were all asking, 'Can I have that bread that's left over?' "

When you make sandwiches with a brioche you need to use material like terry cloth that's thick and that holds water to put the bread in to keep the bread moist. You cut the bread, butter each piece, and cover it with the moist cloth until you finish making the sandwiches. It has a velvety flavor to it—it's so soft and delicious. Once you finish making the sandwiches, you put them back in the brioche crust mold and cover it with the brioche crust top.

One 6-pound freshly baked round
    brioche
1 small loaf pumpernickel bread
1 small loaf whole wheat bread
Ham slices
Chicken slices
Turkey slices
Salami slices
Cheese slices

Liver pâté or other meat spread
Egg salad
1 cup (2 sticks) unsalted butter, room
    temperature
One 8-ounce jar mayonnaise
One 8-ounce jar mustard
Radish rose, for garnish
Parsley sprigs, for garnish

Place the brioche in the center of a cutting board. Using a serrated knife, cut the top and bottom off in one round piece (as if opening the top and bottom of a can). Wrap each piece in a separate damp cloth in order to maintain freshness and set aside. Using a bread knife, cut close to the inside crust of the brioche around the edge of the circle. Be careful not to cut into the circle. Hold the knife with the blade parallel to the side crust of the brioche and simply follow the crust. Allow about 1 inch of the white bread to remain attached to the crust. Push the white bread out of the circle of crust from one end. Slice the core or inner circle of the white bread into four equal parts. Place three parts of the bread into a damp terry cloth. Working with the fourth part, cut into $1/4$-inch thick slices, or as thin as you can. Place the slices into the damp terry cloth. Repeat this process with the other three parts of white bread that you have cut from the center of the brioche.

Cut the crusts from the pumpernickel and whole wheat bread and place in a damp terry cloth. After each step, wipe the cutting board clean to prevent crumbs from getting on the sandwiches as they are being prepared. Remove the bottom of the brioche from the terry cloth and place on a serving tray. Next, set the round bread shell on top. Make a sandwich of your choice using the same type of bread for each sandwich. Spread each side of bread with butter followed by mayonnaise or mustard, depending on the cold cut. Cut each sandwich into several triangle pieces. Arrange to fill the bread mold full to the top. Cover the sandwiches placed in the mold with a damp dish towel to prevent the sandwiches from getting hard. Remove the cloth before adding a layer of sandwiches and place back after each layer of sandwiches has been added. After completing all the sandwiches, place the top of the brioche on top. Garnish with a radish rose and the parsley.

Serves 16

Student at work recipe testing.

Cold Salmon Rosettes with Caper Butter

Recipe from the kitchen of Mrs. Martha Hatcher

$^1/_2$ pound smoked salmon

One 2- to 4-ounce jar capers, with
   liquid

$^1/_4$ cup mayonnaise

$^1/_4$ cup sweet relish

1 teaspoon white wine

$^1/_2$ teaspoon salt

$^1/_2$ teaspoon ground white pepper

1 tablespoon chopped fresh dill

1 loaf pumpernickel bread, thinly
   sliced, crusts trimmed

12 sprigs chives, chopped

Cut the salmon into $^1/_2$- to 1-inch-wide pieces. Coil the salmon into rosettes and use decorative toothpicks to hold them in place. Combine the capers, mayonnaise, relish, wine, salt, pepper, and dill in medium bowl and stir until well mixed. Spread the caper butter over a small area of each bread round. Place a salmon rosette in the center of the sauce and garnish with the chopped chives.

Serves 6 to 8

BILL BOYD

Codfish Fritters Bustamante

Recipe from the kitchen of Verna Rose Martin

This indigenous Jamaican starter is said to be Prime Minister Alexander Busta-mante's favorite at the many hosted dinners and banquets he attends. It is great as an hors d'oeuvre for small or large gatherings, formal receptions, or house par-ties. It can be served either as an appetizer or a main dish.

1 pound salt cod

4 scallions, diced

1 large onion, finely diced

4 teaspoons curry powder

1 Scotch bonnet chile, seeds removed
   and finely chopped

3 cups all-purpose flour

2 teaspoons baking powder

1 teaspoon kosher salt

2 cups cold water

$^{1}/_{2}$ to 1 cup vegetable oil

Place the dried codfish in a dish large enough to cover the fish with water for at least 8 hours. Change water every 2 hours. Drain the water and rinse the fish and then place in a pot of boiling water to cover and boil for 10 minutes. Drain, then place the cod in a large bowl filled with cold water. When the cod has cooled, drain. Re-move the skin from the fish by hand and break into small pieces or flakes. Place the cod in a large bowl and add the scallions, onion, curry powder, and chile and stir to combine. Place the flour, baking powder, salt, and cold water in a large bowl and whisk together to make the batter. Add the fish mixture to the batter and stir until well coated. Place $^{1}/_{2}$ cup of the oil in a large skillet over medium-high heat until hot but not smoking. Use a spoon to drop the batter into the oil. Fry each side until golden brown. Add more oil to the pan to fry the remaining fritters as needed. Drain the fritters on paper towels.

8 to 10 fritters

Rumaki (Water Chestnuts Wrapped in Bacon)

Recipe from the kitchen of Mrs. Martha Hatcher

Two 8-ounce small cans water
   chestnuts
20 to 26 slices bacon

One 16-ounce jar honey
Mint sprigs, for garnish

Preheat the oven to 325°F.

   Drain the water chestnuts and place them in a medium bowl. Wrap each water chestnut with a strip of bacon, then insert a toothpick through each water chestnut to hold it together. Place the water chestnuts on a sheet pan and bake for 10 minutes, or until bacon is crispy and golden brown—*not* thoroughly brown. Remove from the oven and brush the water chestnuts with honey. Return the pan to the oven and bake another 5 minutes, or until the honey has a crystal glow. Place the rumaki on a serving tray and garnish with the mint.

Serves 12

Tuna Monte Cristos

Recipe from the kitchen of Mrs. Martha Hatcher

Most Monte Cristos are not seasoned well. These sandwiches always make people smack their lips.

A traditional Monte Cristo sandwich is made with sliced chicken or turkey and cheese, dipped in an egg mixture, and fried in butter until golden brown.

Two 6-ounce cans tuna	2 cups heavy cream
$1/2$ to $3/4$ cup mayonnaise	3 large eggs
1 medium onion, chopped	6 to 8 bread slices
$1/2$ teaspoon salt	$3/4$ stick margarine
$1/4$ teaspoon cayenne	Chopped fresh parsley, for garnish
$1/4$ teaspoon ground white pepper	1 medium lemon, sliced

Combine the tuna, mayonnaise, onion, salt, cayenne, and pepper in a medium bowl. Combine the cream and eggs in a separate medium bowl. Cut the crusts from each slice of bread, cover the bread, and set aside. Evenly spread the tuna mixture over four slices of bread and top each with another slice of bread. Cut each sandwich into four triangle sections. Melt the margarine in a large frying pan over moderate heat. Dip each triangle in the heavy cream mixture, coating both sides of the sandwiches well. Place as many sandwiches that will fit in the pan and brown on both sides. Remove from the pan and drain on paper towels. Arrange the sandwiches on a serving tray, sprinkle the parsley on top, and serve with the lemon slices.

Serves 12 to 16

Tempura

Recipe from the kitchen of Mrs. Martha Hatcher

Tempura is a Japanese dish of batter-dipped vegetables or fish served with soy sauce for dipping. It should be eaten immediately after frying for optimum flavor and crispness.

4 large egg yolks

4 cups pastry flour

Cottonseed oil for frying

3 to 4 pounds large shrimp, peeled and deveined with tails intact

3 to 4 pounds large scallops

2 pounds boneless, skinless chicken breast, cut into 1-inch-thick strips

1 pound zucchini, cut into 1-inch-thick pieces

1 pound yellow squash, cut into 1-inch-thick pieces

1 pound mushrooms, stems removed

1 pound green tomatoes, cut into large wedges

1 pound snow peas

1 head broccoli, cut into florets

1 head cauliflower, cut into florets

$1^1/_2$ cups self-rising flour for dredging

Soy sauce, for serving

To prepare the batter, whisk the egg yolks with 3 cups ice water in a large bowl. Add the pastry flour and mix lightly; do not overmix. The batter will have lumps. Place 3 inches of oil in an electric fryer or deep, heavy pot over medium-high heat and heat to 365°F. Dip the seafood, chicken, and vegetables in the self-rising flour one at a time, then dip into the batter and place in the oil. Fry for about 1 minute, then turn and fry for another minute. Remove the pieces when crisp and light golden brown. Drain on paper towels and serve with soy sauce.

Serves 12 to 14

Black-Eyed Pea Fritters with Cherry Tomato Coulis

Recipe from the kitchen of Georgia Gowan

I first tasted this dish at a book club meeting in Harlem. After we discussed the book, this was served as an appetizer. Nobody could eat just one!

A coulis is a thick puree of fruit or vegetables used as an accompaniment to the fritters.

Coulis

3 tablespoons olive oil

3 tablespoons finely diced shallots

1 Thai or other chile, minced

2 pints cherry tomatoes

$^1/_4$ cup white vinegar

$^1/_4$ cup extra-virgin olive oil

2 tablespoons chopped cilantro

Salt and freshly ground black pepper

Fritters

1 pound dry black-eyed peas, washed
   and soaked overnight in 4 cups
   water

1 teaspoon cumin seeds, toasted

1 cup finely diced red onion

$^1/_4$ teaspoon cayenne pepper

Salt and freshly ground black pepper

2 large eggs

Vegetable oil for frying

To prepare the coulis, heat the olive oil in a medium skillet over medium heat. Add the shallots and chile and sauté until translucent, about two minutes. Set aside. Place the tomatoes in a blender, add the vinegar and extra-virgin olive oil, and puree. Strain into a large bowl. Add the shallot mixture, the cilantro, and salt and pepper to taste.

To prepare the fritters, drain the black-eyed peas and place them in a large pan with fresh water to cover. Rub the black-eyed peas between your palms to remove the outer husks. The husks will float and the peas will sink. Discard the husks and the water. Cook the peas in 2 cups water for each cup of soaked peas for 45 minutes, or until easily mashed with a fork. Drain off any excess water. Puree the peas in a food processor. Transfer to a large bowl, add the cumin, onion, cayenne, salt and black pepper to taste, and the eggs, and mix well.

Heat the vegetable oil to 350°F in a heavy saucepan or electric frying pan. Using a small scoop, drop the fritter batter into the hot oil. Fry until golden brown, 4 to 5 minutes on each side. Serve with the coulis.

Serves 4

Shrimp Dip

Recipe from the kitchens of Mrs. Tommie Jean Clark and Tramel Garner

The family of Joe Garner, vice chairperson of the Abyssinian board of trustees, is well represented in this book. Originally from Ellisville, Mississippi, Joe Garner joined Abyssinian in 1981, and four years later married Tramel, who had been a member of the church since childhood and whose father had served on the deacon board. Their son Jared Garner was born in 1991 and joined the church in 2004.

The entire family—both the New York and the Mississippi branches and all the living generations—is "partial to good cooking." The Garner recipes came from family members and friends in New York and southern Mississippi—his mother, Brunetta Garner, sister, Jo-Ann Garner, and niece, Tramel McMillan, and family friends Walter and Tommie Jean Clark.

One 4-ounce can tiny whole shrimp, rinsed and drained

1 package original Hidden Valley Ranch dressing

One 8-ounce package cream cheese, softened

One 8-ounce container sour cream

Paprika, for garnish

Combine all the ingredients except the paprika in a medium bowl. Sprinkle paprika on top. Cover with plastic and chill for 1 hour before serving.

Makes 2 cups dip

Soups, Stews, and One-Pot Meals

BILL BOYD

Chicken and Groundnut Stew (page 55),
and Sopa Verde (Green Soup) (page 57).

Palm Nut Okra Stew

Recipe from the kitchen of Deacon Joe Jackson

The connection between Southern American and West African cooking really became apparent to me once I started traveling to Africa, and especially after I met my wife. I grew up in Savannah, Georgia. My wife, Ayikailey, is from Ghana. Yet the foods we grew up eating are very similar, especially one-pot dishes like this one. Okra, rice, and tomatoes are prominent in the Gullah (or Geechie) cooking styles of Savannah and in Ghanaian cooking, so I felt a natural affinity for this dish the very first time my mother-in-law, Ma, made it for me.

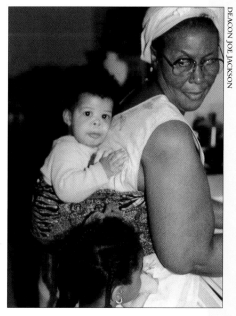

Deacon Joe Jackson learned how to make this recipe for Palm Nut Okra Stew from his wife, Ayikailey's, mother, Caroline Alexia Adamafio, shown here with her granddaughters Caroline and Jasmyn.

Caroline Alexia Adamafio was the consummate mother. She had big beautiful eyes, a captivating smile, and such an aura of comfort about her that everyone affectionately referred to her as Ma, including her husband. Ma's ancestral lineage was Fante, and as a chief's daughter, she was part of the royal family. On one of my visits to Ghana, Ma took my two daughters, Caroline and Jasmyn, and me, to visit the chief's palace in Abakrampa. We were given a tour of the village and information connecting the history of former chiefs to Ma and my two daughters.

Ma lived in Accra, the capital of Ghana, which was within a stone's throw from the State House. It was there that I experienced Ma's unique culinary skill and the joy she felt when presenting something special to her guest from America—me. Not a single sound escaped the small kitchen until Ma completed her masterpiece and summoned me with a cheerful, "It's ready now, come eat." The dish was, to my delight, okra stew with a mix of fish, shellfish, beef, and a variety of spices. Ayikailey and I have attempted to reproduce this dish on numerous occasions. We've come

close, just enough to keep the memory alive. It is Ma's dish—now it's yours to try. Akwaaba!

Serve over rice, fufu, kenkey, or boiled yam. Okra (also known as *gombo*) was brought to the Americas by Africans. Look for palm nuts at specialty or ethnic markets or from grocers that sell African and Caribbean foodstuffs. Jamaican hot chiles and Scotch bonnet chiles come in many colors. It is imperative that the membrane and seeds be removed since these peppers can be very hot. Puree the peppers if you like your stew *very* hot; leave them whole if you do not. Skim off the oil residue on top of the stew. There's no need to add salt to this recipe since it's made with salted meat and smoked fish.

This dish is delicious the first day you make it, and leftovers are even better as the flavors really come together.

1 pound salted beef or pork
2 pounds fresh beef, cubed
5 medium tomatoes, halved
3 medium onions, halved
One 16-ounce can palm nut paste
2 whole Scotch bonnet chiles
2 small smoked herrings, bones
     removed

3 snails (optional)
6 crab legs
Two 9- to 10-ounce boxes whole
     frozen okra
1 medium eggplant, peeled and diced

Place the salted beef or pork in a large pot with 2 cups water, bring to a boil, and cook until tender, about 1 hour. Drain. Place the fresh beef, tomatoes, and onions in another large pot over medium heat and cook for 30 minutes. Remove the tomatoes and onions, place in a food processor or blender, and puree. Add the palmnut paste and 3 cups water to the beef pot and stir thoroughly. Add the tomato mixture and simmer another 20 minutes. Add the salted beef or pork, chiles, herring, and snails, if using, to the pot and simmer 5 minutes longer. Add the crab legs, okra, and eggplant and simmer another 30 minutes, or until heated. Do not overcook the eggplant.

Serves 8 to 10

Spinach Stew

Recipe from the kitchen of Deacon Joe Jackson

If you break open a Jamaican hot chile or Scotch bonnet chile, it will release its seeds, which is where the intense heat of the chile's taste resides. Break it only if you want an especially hot and spicy dish.

Serve this dish with rice and boiled ripe plantains. To make boiled ripe plantains, use one ripe plantain for each individual serving. Peel the plantains and cut each crosswise into three pieces. Place the pieces in a soup pot with just enough water to cover, place over medium heat, and bring to a boil. Boil uncovered until a fork slides easily into the plantains, about 10 minutes. Do not overcook. Pour off the water, or reserve for use in another soup or stew. (Note: this recipe was provided by the editors.)

$1^1/_2$ pounds beef or chicken breast,
    cut into 1-inch-thick cubes
1 cup vegetable or olive oil
2 large onions, chopped
3 large tomatoes, chopped

1 whole Scotch bonnet chile
1 small smoked herring, boned
1 pound fresh leafy green spinach,
    cleaned and torn into pieces

Steam the beef or chicken in a covered pan for 15 to 20 minutes, or until tender. Put aside. Heat the oil in a large skillet over medium heat. Add the onions and tomatoes and stir to break down the tomatoes. Add the whole chile. Do *not* break it open. Simmer for 20 to 30 minutes. Add the herring, beef or chicken, and spinach to the tomato mixture, along with 1 cup water. Simmer for 2 to 3 minutes, until the spinach is tender.

Serves 4 to 6

Chicken and Groundnut Stew

GEORGIA GOWAN

Recipe from the kitchen of Georgia Gowan

This dish brings back fond memories of my dream trip to Africa. I visited Ghana for the first time in November 2002 with the Uptown Sisters Bookclub from Harlem and

Georgia Gowan and children from a village near Agyambera crocodile pond in Ghana, West Africa.

came back with this classic West African recipe. It's delicious, and I ate much of it while I was there. This dish nourishes the body, mind, and spirit, and its African origins give it a special spiritual connection for me.

Groundnut is another name for peanut. Ghana is one of the world's largest growers and exporters of peanuts, which play a large role in African food history and folklore. In Ghana groundnut stew is served with Jollof rice, which is rice steamed in a meat stock with fried minced onion, tomato, and spices. I serve it with simple brown rice. Occasionally I'll add cumin to this dish along with the other spices for a change of flavor.

Brown Rice

1 part rinsed long-grain brown rice to 2 parts water

Place the rice and water in a pot over medium-high heat and bring to a boil uncovered. When the water is level with the top of the rice, reduce the heat to medium. When the rice is the consistency of cooked oats, 3 to 5 minutes later, cover tightly and turn off heat, but leave on the stovetop for 30 to 60 minutes to steam before serving.

2 tablespoons olive oil, more if needed	2 bay leaves
3 pounds chicken thighs, trimmed of excess fat	1/2 teaspoon salt
	1/4 teaspoon cayenne pepper, or to taste
2 medium onions, chopped	3 cups chicken stock
2 garlic cloves, minced	Two 8-ounce cans tomato sauce
1 teaspoon curry powder	3/4 cup smooth unsalted and unsweetened peanut butter
1/2 teaspoon dried thyme	

Heat the oil in a 5-quart Dutch oven over medium-high heat. Add the chicken in batches and cook, turning often, until browned on all sides, about 6 minutes per batch. Add more oil if necessary. Transfer the chicken to a plate and set aside. Add the onions to the pot and sauté, stirring, until lightly browned, about 5 minutes. Add the garlic, curry powder, thyme, bay leaves, salt, and cayenne and cook for 1 minute, stirring. Add the stock and tomato sauce and bring to a simmer.

Return the chicken thighs to the pan, reduce the heat to medium-low, cover tightly, and simmer for about 45 minutes. Remove 1 cup of liquid from the pot and place it in a medium bowl. Add the peanut butter and stir until completely blended. Return the mixture to the pot and cook until heated through, about 2 minutes. Serve over long-grain brown rice.

Serves 6 to 8

Sopa Verde (Green Soup)

Recipe from the kitchen of Ms. Dolores Simanca

This soup can be served as a meal and is especially good during the winter. It calls for chorizo, also known as Spanish sausage, which is a smoked pork sausage seasoned with garlic, chili powder, and other spices and widely used in Latin and Spanish cooking.

2 pounds white baking potatoes,
    peeled and cut into 2-inch-thick
    chunks
2 quarts chicken stock
2 tablespoons olive oil
2 garlic cloves, chopped

1 teaspoon salt, optional
$^1/_2$ teaspoon freshly ground black
    pepper
1 pound fresh kale, stems removed
    and chopped into large pieces
2 chorizo links

Place the potatoes, stock, and oil in a large pot and bring to a boil over high heat. Reduce the heat and simmer until fork-tender. Remove the potatoes from the pot, place in a large bowl, and lightly mash; leave it a little lumpy. Return the potatoes to the pot. Add the garlic, salt, pepper, and kale and cook over medium heat until the kale is tender, 10 to 15 minutes. Add the chorizo and cook another 10 minutes. Remove the sausage and slice it into $^1/_4$-inch-thick pieces. Return the sausage to the soup and cook another 5 minutes. Serve with crusty bread.

Serves 4 to 6

Chef J's Five-Alarm South Bronx Chili

"It's just about done!"—Justin Hay

Recipe from the kitchen of Justin Hay

I started my Abyssinian Baptist Church life as a baby, when I was christened in 1961. I regularly attended church on Sundays with my mother and my Eastern Star grandmother, Nana. I was very close to Nana, and when she passed I stopped attending church for a long while. I later returned to my church family to be baptized and renew the ties, in memory of and out of respect for my grandmother.

Nana and my Aunt Sis were my cooking inspirations. My mom cooks, but her heavy community activism has curtailed her kitchen influence. My dad taught me how to run a kitchen, and I have used his teaching in my professional cooking and catering.

I grew up in the South Bronx when it was being burned down and started making chili back then. I have friends who love hot, hot chili, but I didn't know how to make it. So one cold winter weekend, when I was growing up in the South Bronx, I went to work to make up this recipe. It will make you sweat in a cold winter storm. Serve with milk to soothe the tongue and coat the stomach; water will not do. I'm eating healthier because of my blood pressure and cholesterol level, and enjoy spicy, healthier foods like this chili. This recipe is very spicy.

$^1/_2$ pound ground turkey

$^1/_2$ pound ground beef

$^1/_2$ cup breadcrumbs

1 tablespoon plus 2 teaspoons bajan
   hot pepper sauce

1 tablespoon plus 2 teaspoons hot
   sauce

One 16-ounce can vegetarian baked
   beans

One 16-ounce can kidney beans

One 16-ounce can pork and beans

1 small red or yellow onion, chopped

1 medium green pepper, cored,
   seeded, and chopped

1 medium red pepper, cored, seeded,
   and chopped

Two 8-ounce cans spicy tomato sauce

1 tablespoon chili powder

1 tablespoon jerk sauce

1 teaspoon hot Chinese mustard

1 teaspoon ground black pepper

1 teaspoon cayenne pepper

1 teaspoon crushed red pepper

Combine the ground turkey, beef, breadcrumbs, 2 teaspoons of the bajan hot pepper sauce, and 2 teaspoons of the hot sauce in a large bowl. Cover with foil or plastic wrap and place in the refrigerator to marinate overnight. Brown the meat mixture in a large skillet placed over high heat and set aside. Add the remaining tablespoon of bajan hot pepper sauce and remaining tablespoon of hot sauce. Place the vegetarian beans, kidney beans, and pork and beans in a large pot over low heat. Add the onion, peppers, and tomato sauce, followed by the chili powder, jerk sauce, mustard, black pepper, cayenne, and crushed red pepper. Add the browned meat mixture to the beans and simmer for another 15 minutes.

Serves 6 to 8

Chicken, Roasted Vegetable, and Sweet Potato Potpie

Recipe from the kitchen of Brian Washington-Palmer

"I have a wacky friend from Montreal who has a restaurant that is organic vegetarian with lots of rules. There is one meal served per night. That's it, just one. There is an appetizer and entrée, and the rule of the house is that you must finish your meal. If not, you must pay two dollars. The restaurant matches the two dollars and donates the money to a charity. Dessert can also be or-

Chicken, Roasted Vegetable, and Sweet Potato Potpie.

dered, but if you don't finish it, you are banned from the restaurant for life (or at least until he forgets your face). There are lots of other rules—like no cell phones, and you must come with the proper attitude. He throws people out at whim. I've seen him turn away parties of eight and ten people. The place is decorated with aluminum foil. We took his friend Renée Claude, who is fifty-eight, dancing. He had hurt his back in an accident and had to sleep while sitting up, or so the story goes. I've never seen a fifty-eight-year-old man with a bad back entertain a crowd of club-goers that much—using a curtain and some lady's feathered hat. That's why I like pot pies. No rules. You can throw in whatever you want, including cell phones. You can get crazy—even with a bad back—and you still can have plenty of vegetables."

Bobby Flay, the famous restaurateur, chef, and cookbook author, was the inspiration for this recipe. I like it because it's smooth and creamy and its ingredients are part of the traditional food culture of black people.

In order to get someone to make a potpie, the recipe has to be different from what you'd get prepackaged in the frozen food section. This one is truly different.

Three 8-inch prepared pie crusts with
tops (either a basic pie crust or a
pastry dough crust—my personal
favorite)

2 boiled and diced sweet potatoes

2 small onions, diced

2 small carrots, diced

$1/2$ pound white button mushrooms,
sliced

2 celery ribs, diced

$1/2$ cup plus 2 tablespoons olive oil

2 tablespoons salt

2 tablespoons freshly ground black
pepper

4 cubes of chicken stock in 8 cups
water

6 cups heavy cream

6 boneless, skinless chicken breasts,
sliced

2 tablespoons chipolte or
1 tablespoon cayenne

2 tablespoons honey

2 tablespoons liquid smoke (optional)

Butter, margarine, or condensed milk,
for the pie crust

Preheat the oven to 350°F.

Bake the pie crust bottom according to the package directions. Set aside to
cool while you prepare the filling. Place the sweet potatoes, onions, carrots,
mushrooms, and celery in a large bowl and toss with $1/2$ cup of the olive oil. Add
the salt and pepper and toss. Lay the vegetables on a sheet pan and roast for 25
to 30 minutes, tossing occasionally, until shrivelled and brown. Bring the stock
to a boil in a large saucepan over high heat, and boil until reduced to 6 cups,
about 20 minutes. In a separate saucepan, simmer the cream over medium-high
heat until reduced to 2 cups, about 20 minutes. Heat 2 tablespoons of the oil in
a large sauté pan over medium-high heat. Add the chicken and cook for 8 minutes on each side, or until no longer pink in the middle. Add the cream, chipolte
or cayenne, and honey to the chicken and cook 2 minutes, or until heated
through. Add the vegetables, stock, and liquid smoke, if using, and cook another
2 minutes, or until thick and creamy. Pour the chicken and vegetable mixture
into the bottom crust and cover with the top, uncooked, crust. Brush the top
crust with butter, margarine, or condensed milk to hasten browning. Pierce with
a fork in several places. Bake for 10 to 15 minutes, or until the crust is golden
brown.

Serves 6

Bahamian Seafood Cobbler

BrianWashington-Palmer.

Recipe from the kitchen of Brian Washington-Palmer

This cobbler isn't really from the Bahamas, but it's inspired by the flavors—deep, complex, and varied—of the islands.

For the crust I prefer to use a pastry dough crust. You can buy it in prefrozen sheets—all you need to do is bake it until it rises. This dish will also work with filo dough sheets or sliced sourdough bread. Be creative!

Seafood Cobbler Sauce

2 cups clam juice

³/₄ cup sweet chili sauce

¹/₂ cup fish sauce

¹/₄ cup fresh lime juice

Four 12-ounce cans coconut juice

3 tablespoons curry powder

1 tablespoon ground cumin

3 tablespoons ground coriander

Filling

1 large carrot

1 celery rib

1 teaspoon olive oil

1 large white baking potato, boiled and diced

2 pounds mixed fish (such as whiting, salmon, scallops, shrimp, crabmeat, or bluefish) cut into bite-size chunks

Two 8-inch pastry dough crusts, two 12-inch sheets filo dough, or 4 slices sourdough bread

Preheat the oven to 350°F.

Combine all the cobbler sauce ingredients together in a large bowl. Coarsely chop the carrot and celery, place them in a large pan with the oil, over medium heat and sauté until browned, about 5 minutes. Add the diced potato, then the seafood, and top with the cobbler sauce. Cover and cook until the seafood is cooked through, about 7 minutes. Pour into 4 ovenproof containers, top with the crust, dough, or bread, and bake for 3 minutes, or until the crust is lightly browned on top.

Serves 4

Clam and Sweet Potato Chowder

Recipe from the kitchen of Brian Washington-Palmer

2 cups white wine

2 cups clam juice

4 cups heavy cream

2 tablespoons olive oil

2 onions, chopped

2 celery ribs, cut into $^1/_4$-inch dice

2 tablespoons all-purpose flour

One 2-ounce can clam meat

2 large sweet potatoes, cut into
$^1/_2$-inch dice

1 tablespoon salt

1 tablespoon freshly ground black
pepper

1 tablespoon Tabasco sauce

Combine the wine, clam juice, and 2 cups water in a large pot over high heat, bring to a boil, reduce the heat, and simmer for 15 minutes. Place the cream in a separate pot over medium-high heat, bring to a boil, and cook until reduced by half. Heat the oil in a medium sauté pan over medium heat, add the onions and celery, and sauté until softened, about 2 minutes. Add the flour and cook, stirring, for 2 minutes, or until cooked. Add this mixture to the clam broth and bring to a simmer. Add the clam meat and sweet potatoes and simmer until the potatoes are soft but not mushy, about 10 minutes. Add the cream, reduce the heat to low, and simmer for 5 minutes, or until thoroughly warmed and mixed in. Add the salt, pepper, and Tabasco.

Serves 4

Booba's Saturday Night Special One-Pot Meal

Recipe from the kitchen of Eunice Newkirk

I come from a very large family and am the youngest of fourteen children. While I was growing up many of my sisters and brothers had already left home, but I did grow up with their children—my nieces and nephews—who stayed with us during the week while their parents were working.

I had a very close relationship with my mother, who was also my pastor. Her nickname was Booba, which is similar to the Jewish name for grandmother. At the time of her death, she was a grandmother of five generations: grandmother; great grandmother; great, great grandmother; great, great, great grandmother, and great, great, great, great, great grandmother!

Booba had a passion for cooking. We weren't financially wealthy, but we realized that we were blessed with a wealth that no man could give us—spiritual wealth. This Spam recipe was our Saturday Night Special, which was usually the only time we would eat meat.

This recipe never left me. None of my sisters and brothers remembered how to prepare this dish, and they were surprised that I had. I really find it quite simple—maybe that's why I became a caterer.

2 tablespoons vegetable oil	One 8^{1}/$_{2}$-ounce can peas and carrots
One 12-ounce can Spam, diced	One 4-ounce can evaporated milk
1 tablespoon all-purpose flour	^{1}/$_{4}$ cup ketchup

Heat the oil in a large skillet over medium heat. Add the Spam and flour and cook until the Spam is browned. Add the peas and carrots with their liquid, then add the evaporated milk and ketchup and mix well. Reduce the heat to low and cook for about 15 minutes. Serve over a bed of rice.

Serves 4

Vegetable Soup

Recipe from the kitchen of Venia R. Davis

I learned how to prepare this soup from my mother, and it is especially good in the winter. A neighbor who used to live several floors above me would always say, "I know where and what I will be eating" whenever I would cook this soup. In fact, when she left to go to the store, she would stop at our apartment to inquire about the time dinner would be ready and ask if I needed anything from the store.

$1/2$ red pepper, cored, seeded, and diced

$1/2$ green pepper, cored, seeded, and diced

$1/2$ small onion, diced

4 celery ribs, diced

3 small carrots, sliced

One 28-ounce can crushed or pureed tomatoes

One 1-ounce envelope onion soup mix

$1/2$ teaspoon freshly ground black pepper

$1/2$ teaspoon salt (optional)

$1/4$ pound white cabbage ($1^1/2$ cups), cut into small pieces

One 10-ounce package frozen mixed vegetables

Place the peppers, onion, celery, carrots, and tomatoes in a large saucepan over medium heat. Add the onion soup mix, pepper, salt, if using, and 1 cup water. Bring to a simmer and cook for 30 minutes. Add the cabbage and cook another 20 minutes, or until vegetables are tender. Add the frozen vegetables and cook until the vegetables are heated through, about 10 minutes.

Serves 6 to 8

Meat

Mediterranean Roast Leg of Lamb (page 72)

Braised Lamb Shanks

Recipe from the kitchen of Debra Perry, church usher

I tell my significant other that it took me fifty years to find the "right" mate and I'm going to do all that I can to keep him here at least another fifty years! We are advocates of reducing the threat of high blood pressure and are always on the lookout for tasty, low-sodium meals.

This hearty meat recipe is low in sodium but high in flavor. Serve with couscous, a staple starch of the North African diet.

4 lamb shanks, trimmed of excess fat	Finely grated zest of 1 lemon
2 large garlic cloves, cut into 8 slivers each	$^2/_3$ cup lemon juice
	Salt
2 tablespoons all-purpose flour	Freshly ground black pepper
3 tablespoons vegetable shortening or vegetable oil	4 medium carrots, cut into $^1/_2$-inch pieces
1 bay leaf	8 small onions, sliced into wedges

Cut 4 slits into the flesh of each lamb shank and insert a sliver of garlic in each slit. Lightly dust the shanks with flour. Heat the oil in a heavy pot with a tight-fitting lid over medium heat. Brown the shanks on all sides. Remove all but 1 tablespoon of the fat from the pan. Add the bay leaf, lemon zest, lemon juice, and $^1/_2$ cup water. Season with salt and pepper to taste. Lower the heat, cover, and simmer for $1^1/_2$ to 2 hours, checking for tenderness after $1^1/_2$ hours. Add the carrots and onions during the last 40 minutes of cooking. Transfer the shanks, vegetables, and liquid to a serving platter, and serve.

Serves 4 to 6

Slim-Line Pork Chops with Apple-Raisin Sauce

Recipe from the kitchen of Ms. Betty Anne Syphrette

My grandmother, Dorothy Hamlor, used to make delicious meats and cakes for our family. She gave me this recipe when I was sixteen years old and I cooked it for my first boyfriend.

This well-seasoned, aromatic dish touches nearly all of the food senses (sweet, salty, juicy, crunchy...). The sweet and spice-rich apple-raisin sauce adds even more (fat-free!) flavor and texture.

The lean and clean cuts of pork that are available today are high in protein and nutrients and low in fat.

1 teaspoon olive or sunflower oil, for greasing the pan

6 lean center-cut $^1/_2$-inch-thick pork chops

$^1/_4$ cup cider vinegar or fresh lemon juice

$^1/_4$ cup paprika

2 tablespoons dried oregano, crushed

1 tablespoon chili powder

2 teaspoons minced garlic

2 teaspoons freshly ground black pepper

$^1/_2$ teaspoon cayenne pepper

1 teaspoon dry mustard

2 large egg whites

$1^1/_2$ cups evaporated skim milk

2 cups cornflake crumbs

1 cup garlic-herb breadcrumbs

Apple-Raisin Sauce

$2^1/_4$ cups apple juice

$^1/_2$ cup apple butter

2 apples, cut into $^1/_2$-inch-thick cubes

1 cup raisins

2 tablespoons molasses

1 teaspoon ground cinnamon

$^1/_4$ teaspoon ground nutmeg

$^1/_4$ teaspoon lemon or orange zest

Preheat the oven to 250°F. Oil a large baking pan and set aside.

Trim off excess fat and clean the pork chops by soaking for 10 to 15 minutes in the cider vinegar and $^1/_4$ cup water. Drain off the liquid. Season the pork chops with the paprika, oregano, chili powder, garlic, black pepper, cayenne, and dry mustard. Whisk together the egg whites and evaporated skim milk in a shallow bowl. Combine the cornflake crumbs and breadcrumbs in another shallow bowl. Dip the pork chops into the egg white mixture, one at a time, coating them completely. Then coat both sides of each pork chop with the breadcrumb mixture. Place the pork chops on the pan and cover with foil. Bake for 1 hour and 30 minutes, or until tender.

Meanwhile, make the apple-raisin sauce: Combine the apple juice, apple butter, apples, raisins, molasses, cinnamon, nutmeg, and zest in a medium saucepan and bring to a simmer over very low heat. Simmer for 5 to 10 minutes, or until heated through. Serve warm over the pork chops.

Serves 6

BILL BOYD

Mediterranean Roast Leg of Lamb

Recipe from the kitchen of Ms. Dolores Simanca

I'm Cuban-American and my immediate family settled in the Spanish Harlem neighborhood of Manhattan, where I grew up during the 1950s and 1960s. My family would make this dish instead of roast turkey for Thanksgiving or Christmas dinner.

Have the butcher butterfly the leg of lamb, which means to split the leg of lamb nearly in half lengthwise, leaving the halves hinged on one side to spread open. This type of preparation increases surface area and speeds up cooking.

$^1/_4$ cup plus 2 tablespoons olive oil

6 garlic cloves, finely chopped

2 teaspoons salt

1 teaspoon black pepper

$2^1/_2$ tablespoons ground cumin

$1^1/_2$ teaspoons dried oregano

$^1/_2$ teaspoon ground coriander

One 6- to 7-pound leg of lamb, boned, butterflied, and trimmed of excess fat

1 lime

Preheat the oven to 325°F.

Combine $^1/_4$ cup of the oil, the garlic, salt, pepper, cumin, oregano, and coriander in a medium bowl to make a paste. Spread the paste evenly on both sides of the lamb. The lamb may be cooked immediately or placed in a nonreactive pan or dish, covered with plastic wrap, and refrigerated to marinate for 1 to 2 hours. Heat the remaining 2 tablespoons oil in a large skillet over high heat. Add the lamb and brown on all sides, about 10 minutes total. Transfer the lamb to a roasting pan and roast for 1 hour, or until an instant-read thermometer reads 160°F. Remove the lamb from the oven, squeeze the juice from the lime over the top, and serve immediately.

Serves 6 to 8

North Carolina-Style Ham Hocks

Fannie Pennington.

Recipe from the kitchen of Hattie Pennington

I'm nearly ninety now, so I don't cook very often. But if I want ham hocks, I know how to make them. I always make them in my iron pot. This recipe came from my mama, Hattie, who was born and raised in rural Macon, North Carolina. She married Papa and moved up north to New York with him. Mama always served this with hot cornbread and butter. Papa loved her ham hocks, and so did the rest of our family. Papa would always say, "Make sure to drink that juice. It's good for you. That is pot lickin' juice."

4 smoked ham hocks
2 slices salt pork
1 medium onion, chopped
2 garlic cloves, minced
2 bunches kale, stalks off

1 red bell pepper, cored, seeded, and
  quartered
4 small white turnips, quartered
Black pepper

Place the ham hocks and salt pork in a pot with 8 quarts water and bring to a boil over high heat. Remove the salt pork when desired saltiness is reached. Add the onion and garlic and boil for $1^1/2$ hours, or until the vegetables are tender. Add the kale, red pepper, and turnips. Season with pepper to taste, and simmer until the kale is tender. The total cooking time will be 2 to $2^1/2$ hours.

Serves 6 to 8

Chef J's Chops Italian

Recipe from the kitchen of Justin Hay

I'm the new generation cook in the Hay family. My family heritage is based in Virginia and Jamaica. My passion for cooking comes from my father, who ran kitchens, and my Southern grandmother and Jamaican grandaunt, Sis.

One night I decided to make pork chops, but I didn't want them the usual way. I also had a taste for Italian food. I decided a new recipe was in order! I often make up meals on the fly, based on my mood and the ingredients on hand in my kitchen.

Chef J serves this Italian-inspired dish with vegetables in season, potatoes, and mozzarella-garlic bread with an olive oil dip on the side, and, always, with a salad.

3 tablespoons crushed garlic

$1/2$ cup fresh lemon juice

Four to six $1^1/2$-inch-thick lean center-cut pork chops

One 8-ounce container Italian breadcrumbs

1 tablespoon garlic powder

1 tablespoon freshly ground black pepper

4 to 6 medium red potatoes, sliced

One 8-ounce can low-sugar tomato sauce

One 26-ounce jar plain spaghetti sauce

1 large white button mushroom, sliced into 10 pieces

1 small red or yellow onion, chopped

1 small green pepper, cored, seeded, and chopped

1 small red pepper, cored, seeded, and chopped

1 to 2 tablespoons Italian seasoning

Combine 2 tablespoons of the crushed garlic with the lemon juice and enough water to cover the chops in a medium bowl. Place the pork chops in a deep dish and pour the liquid over them. Cover with plastic and place in the refrigerator to marinate overnight.

Preheat the oven to 350°F.

Combine the breadcrumbs, garlic powder, and black pepper in a small bowl. Remove the chops from the marinade and place them in a large baking dish. Coat the chops with the breadcrumb mixture. Spread the potatoes over the chops and cover with foil. Bake for 30 minutes, then remove the foil.

Meanwhile, prepare the sauce: Pour the tomato sauce and spaghetti sauce in a large saucepan over medium heat. Add the remaining 1 tablespoon garlic, half of the mushroom slices, half of the chopped onion, and half of the green and red peppers. Bring to a simmer, reduce the heat to low, and cook, stirring occasionally, until vegetables soften. Pour the sauce over the chops, cover with the foil again, and bake for 15 minutes longer. Garnish with the remaining vegetables and the Italian seasoning.

Serves 4 to 6

BOB GORE

Student recipe tester.

Ma Eartha's Meatloaf

Recipe from the kitchen of Londel Davis

My mother was the inspiration for this recipe. She enjoyed cooking and always put so much love and soul into whatever she made. Growing up, my family often ate meatloaf for Sunday dinner. Now it's one of the entrées on my Sunday buffet menu. This is a basic meatloaf recipe, but I've modified it somewhat by adding more spice.

Londel Davis.

This meatloaf not only tastes good, it looks good, so the presentation will complement any special occasion.

1 tablespoon Worcestershire sauce

1 tablespoon prepared Dijon mustard

1 tablespoon chopped fresh thyme

1 tablespoon chopped fresh parsley

1 tablespoon seasoned salt

$^1/_4$ teaspoon freshly ground black pepper

1 garlic clove, minced

$^1/_2$ teaspoon paprika

1 large egg

2 pounds ground beef

2 teaspoons vegetable oil

$^1/_2$ onion, diced

$^1/_2$ medium red pepper, cored, seeded, and diced

$^1/_2$ medium green pepper, cored, seeded, and diced

2 slices white bread, cubed

Preheat the oven to 350°F.

Combine the Worcestershire sauce, mustard, thyme, parsley, seasoned salt, pepper, garlic, paprika, and egg in a large bowl and mix in the ground beef. Heat the oil in a medium skillet over medium heat. Add the onion and peppers and sauté until softened, about 2 to 3 minutes. Remove to a plate to cool. Combine the sautéed onion and peppers with the bread cubes, then add to the ground beef mixture. Place in an ungreased 9-inch loaf pan and bake for 45 to 60 minutes, or until loaf is firm.

Serves 6

BILL BOYD

Lamb Tagine Harlem-Style

Brian Washington-Palmer.

Recipe from the kitchen of Brian Washington-Palmer

Now, to be honest, everyone has an angle. So when I opened my restaurant, Native, my angle was "all worlds cuisine." But no one knew what that meant, and we didn't either.

One client called it "food from around the world."

I said, "That's so boring."

Then she said, "Ethno-Latin-Pan-Asian fusion."

I tried.

"I don't get it," she said. "Cuisine influenced by native cultures?"

That, in turn, started an argument over native vs. indigenous, and didn't I know that we black people are the true natives and was I including the Indians, and I better acknowledge them, 'cause if not I was exploiting...I hung up. I figured she was more interested in arguing than eating. So my new new slogan was French-Moroccan-Caribbean cuisine. So I needed a few dishes. And I love lamb. So it was Lamb Tagine Harlem-Style.

"Why are you trying to be Moroccan?" my sister Lisa asked me.

"Because it's my angle," I replied.

8 lamb shanks

2 teaspoons fresh thyme

2 teaspoons fresh rosemary

2 tablespoons onion powder

2 tablespoons garlic powder

1 tablespoon Knorr beef stock or
    1 beef bouillon cube

One 16-ounce jar thick and chunky
    marinara sauce

Olives, for garnish

Orange slices, for garnish

Blanched almonds, for garnish

Put the lamb shanks in a large pot over medium heat and add water to cover, plus an additional 2 cups. Add the thyme, rosemary, onion powder, garlic powder, and beef stock, bring to a simmer, and cook for 2 hours. At this point the meat should practically fall off the bone; if it doesn't, cook it another 30 minutes. The stock should have a nice rich brothy flavor. Add the marinara sauce and cook for another 30 minutes, until the sauce is very thick.

Serve over rice or couscous and garnish with olives, orange slices, and blanched almonds.

Serves 4

Grilled Sirloin with Dominican Creole Sauce

Recipe from the kitchen of Brian Washington-Palmer

I didn't know what Dominican was until I moved to New York. Being a California native, my only Spanish brothers and sisters were from Mexico. When I set up shop in Washington Heights, I was thrilled to encounter a sea of brown faces. These people are so cosmopolitan I thought, they speak Spanish and can do a mean salsa, too. Once at an impromptu street dance when a kindly grandmotherly type pulled me from the crowd, I pretended to salsa, then I made the mistake of saying I could dance like a Puerto Rican and I didn't want to tire her out. Oops! She let me know she was no Puerto Rican and this was not salsa but merengue. Then grandma let it rip with twirls and hips, and hair and back flips (okay, so no back flips), all in keeping with the spicy beat. She got cheers, and I was mortified. Needless to say, my salsa stays with my burrito. She soothed my embarrassment with this great steak. I added a Creole accent to this dish to remind myself that no matter what the language or the age, we all got a little spice inside. This dish can be served with mashed potatoes or rice.

Grilled Sirloin with Dominican Creole Sauce.

Creole Sauce

2 garlic cloves

1 teaspoon dried oregano

$^1/_2$ teaspoon salt

$^1/_2$ teaspoon ground pepper

2 teaspoons vegetable oil

1 small onion, finely chopped

1 mild jalapeño chile, finely chopped

1 small tomato, seeded and finely
   chopped

$^1/_4$ cup green olives, pitted

1 tablespoon capers, drained

$2^1/_2$ cups fish stock, clam juice, or
   shellfish stock

1 cup coarsely chopped green beans

1 cup diced butternut or other winter
   squash

$^1/_4$ bunch cilantro leaves

1 tablespoon vegetable oil

Four 10-ounce sirloin
   steaks

1 tablespoon salt

$1^1/_2$ teaspoons freshly ground black
   pepper

3 to 4 cups cooked white, long grain
   rice

To make the Creole Sauce, mash the garlic using a mortar and pestle with the oregano, salt, and pepper. Heat the vegetable oil in a large saucepan over medium-high heat. Add the onion, garlic mixture, chile, and tomato and sauté for 1 minute, or until the garlic smells pungent and the chile and tomatoes are paste. Add the olives, capers, and fish stock, and simmer for 5 minutes. Add the green beans and squash and cook for another 5 minutes.

While the sauce is simmering, preheat the oven to 350°F.

Heat the vegetable oil in a large skillet over medium heat. When the pan is very hot, add the steaks. Sprinkle with salt and pepper and cook until the steaks are crisp on both sides, about 2 to 3 minutes per side. Transfer to the oven and cook until medium, about 7 minutes or until internal temperature reaches 140°. Serve with rice or mashed potatoes on the side and Creole Sauce on top. Garnish with cilantro.

Serves 4

Chitterlings

Recipe from the kitchen of Reverend
Kevin R. Johnson

This recipe is from my grandmother, Sedalia Johnson, of Austin, Texas. The key to cooking chitterlings is in cleaning them and keeping the unappetizing odor down. They're sold cleaned, but you'll still need to clean them carefully yourself. To clean chitterlings, pull off all the fatty tissue and rinse well with warm water, running your fingers down the chitterlings. Adding the whole potato helps kill some of the odor.

5-pound bucket chitterlings, cleaned
   well and rinsed
$\frac{1}{2}$ medium onion
1 teaspoon crushed red pepper
   (optional)

1 teaspoon ground black pepper
1 teaspoon salt
1 whole large baking potato

Put the chitterlings in a large pot and add all the remaining ingredients.

Add water just to cover (they will make more water as they cook). Place the pot over high heat, bring to a boil, then reduce the heat to medium.

Simmer for 4 hours, or until soft, stirring occasionally so they will not stick to the pot.

Serves 4 to 6

Poultry and Egg Dishes

Pan-Seared Duck with Parmesan Risotto
and Orange-Tomatillo Sauce (page 104).

Chicken Chasseur

Recipe from the kitchen of Verna Rose Martin

I grew up in a Jamaican family in England. This recipe hails from France, where I studied classic French culinary techniques.

Easy to make.

2 small Cornish hens or 1 medium whole chicken, 3 pounds total weight

$^1/_4$ cup white vinegar

1 cup plus 1$^1/_2$ teaspoons all-purpose flour

1 teaspoon kosher salt

1 teaspoon ground white pepper

2 tablespoons unsalted butter

1 medium onion, thinly sliced

$^1/_2$ cup white wine

1 large tomato, cut into $^1/_4$-inch cubes

$^1/_4$ cup finely chopped fresh parsley

5 medium white button mushrooms, sliced

1 cup canned chicken stock

$^1/_4$ teaspoon gravy browning sauce

Cut each Cornish hen in half, or if using chicken, cut it into 8 pieces (2 legs, 2 thighs, 2 wings, 2 breasts), remove and discard the skin and place in a colander. Combine $^1/_4$ cup cold water with the vinegar in a measuring cup and pour it over the chicken. Rinse and pat dry. Combine 1 cup of the flour, the salt, and white pepper in a small bowl. Coat the hens or chicken pieces with the flour mixture. Heat the butter in a large skillet over medium-high heat until it starts to foam. Brown the hens or chicken pieces for 3 minutes on each side. Remove from the pan and set aside. Add the onions to the pan and sauté for 1 minute. Add the remaining 1$^1/_2$ teaspoons flour, the wine, tomato, parsley, mushrooms, chicken stock, and gravy browning sauce. Return the hens or chicken pieces to the pan, cover, bring to a simmer, and cook for 30 to 35 minutes, or until done.

Serves 4

Baked Chicken Legs Inspiration

Recipe from the kitchen of Ms. Valerie N. Jackson

In 2002, my doctor told me that my blood pressure was very high. He advised me to eliminate salt and starches and to reduce my fat and sugar intake. I went home and started experimenting with new ways to prepare chicken legs, which I love. I thought this dish wasn't going to taste good, because it had no salt, but to my surprise, it was tasty! Now I cook chicken legs this way all the time. When I went back to my doctor for a follow-up visit, he was amazed at how much my blood pressure had gone down.

6 chicken drumsticks
6 chicken thighs

1 tablespoon garlic powder

Preheat the oven to 350°F.

Place the drumsticks and thighs in a large baking dish and sprinkle both sides with garlic powder. Cover with foil and place in the refrigerator to marinate for 30 minutes. Bake uncovered for 1 hour or until juices are clear when pierced or thermometer reads 160°F. Increase the oven temperature to 400°F and bake for 5 minutes, until the chicken is crispy brown. Turn the pieces over and brown the other side about 6 to 9 minutes.

Serves 6

Soulful Chicken "Stir-Fry"

Recipe from the kitchen of Ms. Lovelle A. Clark

I love Chinese food, and I was inspired by all the Chinese restaurants around the country I've ever been to to make my own Chinese food with what I like to call an "African American soul food twist."

Making stir-fries is a great way to get lots of fresh vegetables into your diet. For a low-fat, low-calorie alternative, remove the skin from the chicken pieces and instead of frying, add the uncooked chicken strips to the vegetable mix and stir-fry them all together.

$^1/_2$ cup all-purpose flour

$^1/_2$ teaspoon salt

$^1/_4$ teaspoon freshly ground pepper

2 boneless, skinless chicken breasts, cut into 2-inch strips

$^1/_4$ cup canola or sunflower oil

1 tablespoon olive oil

8 medium to large fresh mushrooms, chopped into 1-inch pieces

$^3/_4$ pound broccoli, cut into florets

$^1/_2$ medium onion, diced

Place the flour, salt, and pepper in a large container. Add the chicken pieces and coat them with the flour mixture. Heat the canola oil in a large skillet over high heat. Add the chicken pieces and fry until golden brown. Remove from the heat and place on paper towels to drain. Heat the olive oil in a large sauté pan over high heat. Add the mushrooms, broccoli, and onion. Cover the pan and heat over medium-low heat. Add salt and pepper to taste and $^1/_4$ cup water. Add the chicken pieces to the vegetable mixture along with another $^1/_4$ cup water. Cook over medium heat, stirring once or twice, until cooked. Serve over rice.

Serves 4 to 6

Smothered Chicken

Recipe from the kitchen of Sylvia Woods

Sylvia Woods of Sylvia's Restaurant has been called the "Queen of Soul Food," and this is one of her family's signature recipes.

Two 3^1/$_2$-pound frying chickens, each cut into 8 pieces

1 tablespoon plus 1 teaspoon salt

1 tablespoon plus 1 teaspoon freshly ground black pepper

2 cups plus 2 tablespoons all-purpose flour

^{1}/$_2$ cup vegetable oil for frying, plus more if needed

2 large onions, coarsely chopped

2 green peppers, cored, seeded, and coarsely chopped

2 celery ribs, coarsely chopped

Trim the excess fat from the chicken pieces and sprinkle them with 1 teaspoon of the salt and 1 teaspoon of the pepper. Season 2 cups of the flour with the remaining 1 tablespoon salt and 1 tablespoon pepper. Dredge the chicken pieces in the flour to coat all sides. Shake off any excess flour.

Heat the oil in a deep heavy skillet (cast iron is perfect) over medium-high heat until the edge of a chicken piece dipped into the oil gives off a lively sizzle. Add as many chicken pieces to the skillet as will fit without touching. Fry until the pieces are browned on all sides, about 6 minutes total. Adjust the heat as necessary to keep a lively sizzle without over browning. Remove the fried chicken to paper towels to drain and repeat with the remaining pieces, adding more oil if needed.

Pour off all but 4 tablespoons of the drippings from the skillet. Reduce the heat to medium and add the onions, peppers, and celery to the skillet. Cook, stirring occasionally, until lightly browned and tender, about 10 minutes. Move the vegetables to one side of the skillet and sprinkle the remaining 2 tablespoons flour over the other side of the skillet. Cook the flour until golden brown, stirring constantly, taking care not to let the flour burn. Slowly pour in 2 cups water and stir until the gravy is smooth.

Divide the chicken between 2 heavy skillets with lids or place them all in a large Dutch oven. Top with the gravy and vegetables and cover tightly. Place over medium heat, bring to a simmer, reduce the heat to low, and cook about 15 minutes, or until the vegetables are tender and the chicken is cooked through. Check the seasoning and add salt and pepper as necessary. Serve the chicken with some of the gravy and vegetables over each piece. Pass extra gravy at the table.

Serves 4

Simple Roast Chicken

Recipe from the kitchen of Carole Darden-Lloyd, co-author with her sister Norma of the twenty-plus-year-old classic cookbook Spoonbread and Strawberry Wine

As African Americans, we place a vital signature on everything we do. This signature becomes so distinctive that we see it copied throughout the world in ways that surprise even us. When any other race talks about "soul," it has a completely different meaning. We can see when soul is lacking, and when it's there. Soul is unifying. What attracted me to Abyssinian was that soulfulness.

Carol Darden-Lloyd.

Soul food, our unique contribution to the American culinary landscape, is imbued with a similar distinction. An easy description of soul food would list any number of foods and how they're prepared. The more complex definition is what African Americans share together while they eat—the camaraderie and the community that's inspired by the food.

Back in the day, a roast chicken frequently graced the Sunday dinner table of many families. It was a special meal that was looked forward to with great anticipation. For me it remains an elegant and simple centerpiece for a meal worthy of anticipation.

1 small (about 2^1/$_2$-pound) chicken
2 teaspoons poultry seasoning
1 teaspoon Vegesal vegetable
   seasoning or other seasoning salt
1 teaspoon paprika

^{1}/$_2$ cup chicken stock
^{1}/$_4$ teaspoon salt
^{1}/$_4$ teaspoon freshly ground black
   pepper

Preheat the oven to 400°F.

Loosen the skin of the chicken without tearing it and trim the excess fat. Clean the chicken thoroughly, rinsing inside and out and patting dry. Place the chicken in a large ovenproof skillet. Sprinkle with the poultry seasoning, Vegesal, and paprika. Place in the oven and roast for 1 hour. Do not baste. Remove from the oven, then baste the chicken. Place it back in the oven and roast an additional 5 minutes, or until golden brown. Remove the chicken from the oven and place it on a small platter. Sit the skillet on a burner over high heat, making sure to use an oven mitt. Add the chicken stock and bring to a boil. Scrape up any particles that may be clinging to the skillet to make an essence. Lower heat and simmer for 4 to 5 minutes. Add the salt and pepper. Strain the liquid into a small bowl. Carve the chicken and serve with the essence spooned on top. If you wish to make gravy, add an additional cup of stock to the pan. Bring the mixture to a boil. Put 2 tablespoons of flour in a jar with a lid. Add $^3/_4$ cup water, screw the lid on tightly, and shake vigorously until smooth. Slowly add flour mixture to the boiling liquid, stirring constantly. Add only enough flour mixture to reach a desired consistency. Lower heat and simmer 8 to 10 minutes. Adjust seasonings and serve.

Serves 4

BILL BOYD

Joyce's Bajan Curry Chicken

Recipe from the kitchen of Joyce Pinder-Haynes

This dish can be paired with yellow rice and Cuban Black Beans (page 140) or Sautéed Kale (page 164).

2 tablespoons Jamaican-style yellow
    curry powder
2 tablespoons poultry seasoning
2 tablespoons seasoned salt
Leaves from 3 sprigs fresh thyme
2 pounds chicken meat, from a whole
    chicken or breasts, cut into 2-inch
    pieces

$^1/_4$ cup vegetable oil
$^1/_2$ Scotch bonnet chile, seeded and
    chopped
1 large onion, thinly sliced
3 garlic cloves, chopped
1 cup low-sodium chicken stock
Salt and freshly ground black pepper

BILL BOYD

Combine the curry, poultry seasoning, seasoned salt, and thyme in a small bowl. Rub the seasonings all over the chicken. Heat the oil in a large skillet over high heat. Add the chicken and sauté. Remove chicken to a plate to keep warm. Sauté the chile, onion, and garlic until soft, about 2 minutes. Return chicken to pan. Add the broth. Stir to prevent sticking. Cover and simmer 15 minutes, or until chicken is done. Season with salt and pepper to taste.

Serves 6

Garlic Fried Chicken

Recipe from the kitchen of Ms. Dolores Simanca

Like most Cubans, I was baptized and raised a Catholic. Some longtime friends of mine who were members of Abyssinian knew that I had not been involved in the Catholic church for many years and suggested I attend their service, which I did. I fell in love with the spirit-moving choir, the warmth of its members, and the gospel preached by Reverend Butts as I've never heard the gospel before. It was a spiritual awakening. I attended services at Abyssinian for over ten years before I took the step and converted. It's been an ongoing spiritual joy ever since.

3 garlic cloves, minced

1 teaspoon salt

1 teaspoon freshly ground black pepper

1 teaspoon dried oregano

1 teaspoon ground cumin

1 teaspoon olive oil

1 teaspoon white vinegar

2 to 3 pounds chicken thighs and drumsticks

Mix the garlic, salt, pepper, oregano, cumin, oil, and vinegar into a paste and smear all over the chicken parts. Place in a large bowl, cover with plastic, and place in the refrigerator to marinate overnight. Turn oven to broil. Place chicken on drip pan and broil for 15 minutes skin side up. Turn chicken over and broil 15 minutes or until juices run clear when pierced.

Serves 4 to 6

Harlemade Brown Paper Bag Fried Chicken

MINDY STRICKE

Kevin McGruder.

Recipe from the kitchen of Kevin McGruder

This recipe was printed on beautifully designed placemats, a sell-out item in Harlemade, a popular Harlem gift store that features merchandise celebrating contemporary Harlem and nostalgic items reflecting Harlem's fabled past. Harlemade prides itself on its warm yet modern feeling and is committed to offering its customers new African American cultural products on a monthly basis.

Kevin McGruder, co-owner of Harlemade, is a member of the archives ministry at Abyssinian, a graduate of Columbia University's business school, former owner of Home to Harlem gift shop, and a Harlem resident who has worked in community development for many years.

In this fried chicken recipe, flour is placed in a brown paper bag and the chicken is added to coat before frying.

One 3-pound fryer chicken, cut up
1 teaspoon salt
$^1/_2$ teaspoon freshly ground black pepper

1 teaspoon garlic powder
1 teaspoon poultry seasoning
2 cups vegetable oil
$1^1/_2$ cups all-purpose flour

Clean, rinse, and dry the chicken. Season the chicken with the salt, pepper, garlic powder, and poultry seasoning. Place in a large bowl, cover, and set aside for 20 minutes. Heat the oil in large skillet over medium-high heat. Place the flour in a medium brown paper bag. Place 3 or 4 chicken pieces in the bag at a time and shake to coat. Dust off any excess flour, place the chicken pieces in the skillet in batches, and fry until golden brown on all sides, 20 to 25 minutes.

Serves 6 to 8

BILL BOYD

Chicken Fricassee with Drop Dumplings

Recipe from the kitchen of Carole Darden-Lloyd

Chicken Fricassee rivaled roast chicken in our family. And it's great served with drop dumplings. At one point while I was growing up we raised chickens in our backyard, so the recipe first included catching a chicken. It was considered a special treat if an egg was found in the cavity. We would add the egg to the pot just before dropping in the dumplings.

Chicken Fricassee

One 3-pound chicken, skin and
　　excess fat removed
2 teaspoons salt or Vegesal vegetable
　　seasoning
$1/2$ teaspoon freshly ground black
　　pepper
3 medium carrots, cut in half
4 large celery ribs, including leaves,
　　cut into thirds
1 medium onion, quartered
1 bay leaf
2 large whole garlic cloves, peeled
2 pinches dried rosemary
3 to 4 cups chicken stock

Drop Dumplings

1 cup all-purpose flour
2 teaspoons baking powder
$1^1/2$ tablespoons Smart Balance
　　spread, melted
$1/2$ teaspoon salted buttery spread
$1/3$ cup low-fat milk or chicken stock

Cut the chicken into 8 pieces. Season with the salt and pepper, rubbing it all over the chicken. Place the chicken in a large pan with a lid. Add the carrots, celery, onion, bay leaf, garlic, and rosemary. Add the stock, to almost cover the chicken. Bring to a boil over high heat, then reduce the heat and simmer, covered, for 45 minutes. Meanwhile, make the dumplings: Combine the flour and baking powder in a small bowl. Add the melted Smart Balance buttery spread, and milk or stock, and stir until well moistened. The batter will be stiff. Drop by rounded tablespoonfuls into the simmering liquid in and around the chicken fricassee. Partially cover and cook for 16 to 18 minutes. Remove the carrots, celery, onion, and garlic cloves with a slotted spoon and place in a blender. Add $1^1/_2$ cups of the cooking broth, and blend until smooth. Pour the mixture back into the pot and adjust the seasoning. Simmer for another 15 minutes, or until the chicken is very tender.

Serves 4

Turkey and Barbecue Beans

Recipe from the kitchen of C. Vernon Mason

When my wife, Thelma, and I joined Abyssinian in the mid 1970s, we had only one child. Our pastor at the time was Dr. Samuel DeWitt Proctor, former university president, educator, pastor extraordinaire, and mentor to Dr. Martin Luther King Jr. He was a phenomenal person. When he passed, his mentoring was mentioned in his eulogy; he had encouraged three hundred African Americans to get—and who got!—their doctorates.

Although Dr. Proctor possessed stellar credentials, he wasn't a stuffy academic or an uptight theologian. He was a great storyteller, and he had a sense of humor you couldn't imagine. We had only been attending Abyssinian a few months when Dr. Proctor told my wife and me, "Mason! Y'all don't have enough children!" Although that was a funny statement, it was prophetic because two years later our second daughter was born, and two years after that we had a son. We used to joke with Dr. Proctor and tell him that he was the reason we had these children.

When you raise your kids at Abyssinian you inherit an extended family that helps nurture them. Our children would not be where they are now if it had not been for that extended family. The church family has been concerned about our kids from birth. There's not a young person at Abyssinian who successfully goes through college or does something else significant without the input of the extended family. Even today, almost thirty years later, there's a continued interest that motivates people to ask us how our children are doing.

In our family we wouldn't schedule anything on Sunday because the entire day was devoted to Abyssinian. Because everyone was involved, you never gave a thought to how much time you were spending at the church. I used to be a trustee, and I also worked as a server in the kitchen. Now I'm a deacon, and Thelma is president of the Deaconess Board. My wife brought this recipe back from her mother Debra's home in Texas.

3 tablespoons vegetable oil

1 pound ground turkey

1 medium onion, chopped

1 medium green pepper, cored,
    seeded, and chopped

1 garlic clove, chopped

Two 28-ounce cans barbecue beans

Heat 2 tablespoons of the oil in a large skillet over medium-high heat. Add the ground turkey and sauté until medium-brown, about 5 minutes. Remove the turkey from the pan to a large plate. Add the remaining oil, onion, green pepper, and garlic to the pan, and cook for 2 to 3 minutes, or until the vegetables soften. Return the turkey to the pan, add the beans, and cook for 5 to 7 minutes to warm through.

Serves 8 to 10

Turkey Pasta Sauce

Recipe from the kitchen of Tara Posey

This sauce is a winner! I like to make a big pot of it and share it with my close neighbors. They absolutely love it! Nobody believes me when I tell them it's made with ground turkey and not ground beef.

This sauce tastes even better the next day once the flavors have had a chance to seep in. And ground turkey has less fat and cholesterol than ground beef.

2 tablespoons olive oil

1 pound ground turkey

1 pound Italian-style turkey sausage, removed from casing

1 large onion, chopped

1/2 cup diced green pepper

1/2 cup diced red pepper

3 large garlic cloves, minced

4 white button mushrooms, sliced

One 28-ounce can crushed tomatoes with basil

One 8-ounce can tomato paste with Italian seasonings

Two 8-ounce cans tomato sauce with Italian seasonings

1/2 teaspoon dried oregano

1/2 teaspoon dried basil

1/2 teaspoon dried thyme

1/2 teaspoon dried marjoram

1/2 cup chopped fresh flat-leaf parsley

3 dashes Tabasco or hot pepper sauce

Salt

Freshly ground black pepper

Heat the oil in a large saucepan over high heat. Add the ground turkey and sausage and sauté for 15 minutes, or until browned. Pour off all but 1 tablespoon excess oil. Add the onion, peppers, and garlic. Reduce the heat to medium and cook until the vegetables have softened. Add the mushrooms, crushed tomatoes, tomato paste, tomato sauce, oregano, basil, thyme, marjoram, parsley, and Tabasco. Bring to a simmer and cook, covered, for 1 hour and 30 minutes, or until done. Season with salt and pepper to taste. Serve over your choice of pasta.

Serves 4 to 6

Turkey Enchiladas

Recipe from the kitchen of Jean B. Riggins

When I retired two years ago, I decided to eat healthier and enjoy life. So I took all of my recipes, cut out the beef, and substituted turkey, or in some cases used no meat at all. I make these often because my neighbors love them!

Mexican cooking ingredients are available at some grocery stores and ethnic markets.

3 tablespoons olive oil

1 medium white onion, diced

2 to 3 green onions, $^1/_4$ inch slices

$1^1/_2$ pounds ground turkey (white meat)

Two 1.25- or 1.75-ounce packages taco seasoning mix

1 medium tomato, chopped

Two $15^1/_2$-ounce cans enchilada sauce

12 corn tortillas

$1^1/_2$ cups grated cheddar cheese

One $3^1/_2$-ounce can sliced black olives

Preheat the oven to 375°F. Heat 1 tablespoon of the oil in a large skillet. Add $^3/_4$ cup of the onions and $^1/_2$ cup of the green onions and sauté until onions are wilted. Add the ground turkey and cook until browned. Add the seasoning mix, $^1/_2$ cup of the tomatoes, and 1 can of the enchilada sauce. Remove from the heat and set aside. Heat the remaining 2 tablespoons oil in a large nonstick skillet. Add the tortillas one at a time and fry for 15 seconds on each side, or until the tortillas are very limp. Remove the tortillas to a platter. Spread 1 to 2 tablespoons of the turkey mixture and 1 tablespoon of the cheese over each tortilla, roll them up, and place them in a greased baking pan close to each other, seam side down. Pour the remaining can of enchilada sauce over the tortillas, sprinkle with the remaining cheese, onions, green onions, and the olives. Bake for 25 minutes, or until the cheese melts and the enchiladas are heated through.

Makes 1 dozen

Pan-Seared Duck with Parmesan Risotto and Orange-Tomatillo Sauce

Recipe from the kitchen of Brian Washington-Palmer

My restaurant, Native, in Harlem, is a gathering place for many young émigrés to Harlem like myself. I was raised in California, and the first food for me and my buddies was Mexican—chicken and rice. That, Cheerios™, and pizza were our diet.

When I was younger, I had to cook something for a special event. I wanted to use ingredients that were familiar so my friends would at least try it. "What is close to a burrito, but elegant?" I asked myself. "Duck! It is close to chicken. Risotto is rice." I couldn't get too far from Mexican, hence the tomatillos. And the orange sauce was my version of an enchilada sauce.

This dish became a favorite of my buddies and restaurant clients. It's the basic chicken and rice—upscaled.

In this recipe, start by preparing the sauce and set it aside. Then prepare the risotto and while the wine is reducing, start the duck.

Parmesan Risotto

2 tablespoons olive or vegetable oil

2 cups Arborio rice

$^1/_2$ cup white wine

$3^1/_2$ cups vegetable stock

4 tablespoons Parmesan cheese

1/4 cup heavy cream

4 duck breasts

Salt

Freshly ground black pepper

2 tablespoons vegetable oil

Orange-Tomatillo Sauce

3 cups chicken stock

1 cup rice vinegar

1 cup sugar

3 cups orange juice

4 black peppercorns

5 small to medium tomatillos

2 tablespoons horseradish

2 tablespoons chipotle or Tabasco sauce

2 oranges, peeled, quartered, and sliced $^1/_4$-inch thick, for garnish

To make the the Parmesan Risotto, heat the oil in a large saucepan over medium heat. Add the rice and stir until lightly browned, about 3 minutes. Add the wine and cook until it is almost evaporated. Add half the vegetable stock and cook until the liquid has evaporated. Add the remaining vegetable stock and cook until the rice is cooked through but still firm. (You may not use all the stock.) Add the Parmesan and cream and cook, stirring, for 10 to 15 minutes, or until slightly sticky.

To make the Orange-Tomatillo Sauce, place the chicken stock in a medium saucepan over high heat, bring to a boil, and boil until reduced to 2 cups, about 20 minutes. In a separate saucepan, combine the vinegar and sugar, place over medium heat, bring to a boil, then reduce the heat and simmer, stirring, until the sugar is dissolved, about 10 minutes. Increase the heat to high, add the orange juice and peppercorns, and boil until reduced to 2 cups, about 10 minutes. In the last 2 minutes of cooking add the tomatillos. Add the chicken stock, horseradish, and chipotle or Tabasco sauce and stir until smooth.

To make the duck, preheat the oven to 350°F. Sprinkle salt and pepper on both sides of the duck breasts. Heat the oil in a large ovenproof skillet over high heat. Place the duck skin side down in the pan and cook until slightly crisp, about 2 minutes. Turn the duck, transfer to the oven, and cook for 10 minutes, or until the duck is medium done.

To serve, spoon some Parmesan Risotto on individual serving plates, slice the duck, and arrange the pieces around the risotto. Spoon on the Orange-Tomatillo Sauce, and serve.

Serves 4

Roast Duckling à L'Orange

Recipe from the kitchen of Deaconess Jessie Green

Two 4-pound ducklings

2 teaspoons salt

1 cup orange juice

2 tablespoons unsalted butter

1 box cornbread stuffing or other
    stuffing of your choice, prepared
    per box instructions

Sage leaves, for garnish

Preheat the oven to 325°F.

Cut the necks off the ducklings and leave the skin on. Clean the ducklings and pat them dry. Rub the salt into the cavities and set aside.

Combine the orange juice and butter in a small saucepan over low heat and heat, stirring constantly, until the butter is melted. Remove from the heat. Using a pastry brush, coat the duck cavities with the orange juice mixture.

Lightly fill the ducks' bodies and neck cavities with the stuffing. To close the body cavities, skewer them or sew them with a cord. Use the skewers to pin the neck skin to the backs and the wings to the bodies. Place the ducklings breast side up on the rack of a 12 by 17-inch roasting pan. Brush with the orange juice mixture. Roast uncovered, frequently brushing the ducklings with the orange juice mixture, for 2^1/$_2$ to 3 hours, or until the ducklings test done. To test for doneness, move the leg gently by grasping the end bones—the drumstick thigh joint will move easily. Pour the drippings from the roasting pan into a bowl as they accumulate and reserve to make a gravy. Place the ducklings on a heated platter, remove the skewers or cords, garnish with sage, and serve.

Serves 2

Frittata

Recipe from the Abyssinian kitchen, by Zana Billue and the Student Recipe Testers

The making of this cookbook was a demonstration of how God works in the church. Blessings are always many-sided—those who bless others also receive blessings, and often the blessings ripple out endlessly.

Zana Billue, an experienced culinary arts professional, was hired to test the recipes. She suggested that the church use this project to expose young African Americans to the varied opportunities in the culinary field, in which blacks remain grossly underrepresented. She hired two students from Harlem Tabernacle, a church near Abyssinian, and the other two from the nonprofit organization Careers through Culinary Arts Program (250 West 57th Street, Suite 2015, New York, NY 10107, www.ccapinc.org, 212-974-7111) to help correct that imbalance.

The student recipe testers, Tah'swanna Khali Davis, John Gamble-Jennings, Tiani Watson, and Quiyona Gould, gained valuable experience and summer employment. The church accomplished its mission by making the cookbook part of its ministry to youth and the community and, at the same time, demonstrated good financial stewardship.

A ripple effect of God's blessing through Zana was that the Abyssinian staff was able to dine family-style in the Abyssinian kitchen for several weeks as Zana and the students tested the recipes. Just as Jesus in the feeding of the five thousand set an example, "Gather the pieces that are left over. Let nothing be wasted" on the last day of recipe testing Zana used the food that was left over to bless her hardworking crew with this delicious frittata.

A frittata is like an openfaced omelet that is usually finished in the oven or under a broiler. The following ingredients are a guide, but frittatas can be made with anything, whether they are leftovers or not.

6 large eggs

Salt

Freshly ground black pepper

4 scallions, chopped

5 medium white button mushrooms,
   sliced

1 tablespoon vegetable oil

$^1/_2$ cup shredded mozzarella cheese

Preheat the oven to 375°F.

Beat the eggs in a medium bowl, season to taste with salt and pepper and add the scallions and mushrooms. Heat the oil in a medium ovenproof skillet. Add the egg mixture, and using a rubber spatula, keep bringing the edges to the center of the pan to cook the eggs evenly, about 3 minutes. Just before the eggs set, sprinkle the cheese to cover the eggs evenly. Place in the oven and bake for 5 minutes, or until the cheese melts. The frittata will expand while in the oven, then deflate once it is removed. Cut into quarters and serve immediately.

Serves 4

Zana Billue (center), who tested the recipes for the book on site in the Abyssinian kitchen, with help from a Harlem Sunday school student, John Gamble-Jennings, and Tah'swanna Khali Davis (right) and Tiani Watson (left), students from the Careers through Culinary Arts Program.

Fish and Seafood

Pan-Seared Salmon Salad with Goat Cheese
and Honey Vinaigrette (page 128).

Broiled Catfish in White Clam Sauce

Recipe from the kitchen of Mr. Robert Lawrence Hull

I learned to cook from my mother, Minerva Hull, whose six siblings were all great cooks too. For many years they owned and operated a family catering business headed by my aunt Beatrice Talley, who was an integral part of the church's history and cooking legacy. As a youngster, I spent a lot of time watching my aunt prepare food, and my job often included peeling potatoes and helping pack the food for delivery.

I was motivated to create this recipe by my wife, Barbara, who challenged me to find an interesting new way to prepare fish, and now this recipe is her favorite!

This is a wonderful and more healthful alternative to fried catfish. Serve over white or yellow rice.

1 teaspoon salt

Black pepper

$1/2$ teaspoon garlic powder

$1/2$ teaspoon seafood seasoning

1 teaspoon paprika

4 catfish fillets

4 teaspoons unsalted butter or
    margarine

One 10.5-ounce can white clam sauce

Preheat the oven to broil.

Combine the salt, pepper, garlic powder, seafood seasoning, and paprika in a small bowl. Season each fish fillet with the seasoning mixture. Place the fillets on a greased broiler pan and place 1 teaspoon butter on each fillet. Broil until the fillets are browned on each side, turning once, 5 minutes total. Remove the fish from the broiler and reduce the oven temperature to 325°F. Drain any excess butter from the pan. Pour the clam sauce over the fish, return the fish to the oven, and bake 5 minutes longer, or until heated through. Serve immediately.

Serves 4

Cilantro Fish Cooked in Parchment

Recipe from the kitchen of Debra Perry

My significant other was diagnosed with high blood pressure, so we have been modifying our diets to address his illness. We both love to eat and knew that we would not stay on a diet that wasn't flavorful, so we are always on the hunt for delightful recipes. The real story is in the parchment paper. I always used to forget to purchase the parchment paper and would have to go back to the store to get it at the last minute. Eventually I renamed the dish just so I'd remember to get the parchment paper!

This dish looks great served with brightly colored vegetables. Serve over rice.

Safflower oil for coating the
    parchment
4 large red snapper, cod, flounder, or
    orange roughy fillets
1 teaspoon grated ginger

2 tablespoons sake or rice wine
1 tablespoon fresh lime juice
1 teaspoon lime zest
2 tablespoons minced cilantro
1 teaspoon dark sesame oil

Preheat the oven to 400°F.

Lightly oil four 4 by 8-inch sheets of parchment paper with the oil. Place 1 fillet in the center of each sheet of parchment. Combine the ginger, sake, lime juice, lime zest, cilantro, and sesame oil in a small bowl and spoon some of the mixture over each fillet. Join the edges of the parchment and roll them together to form a packet around the fish. Place in a baking pan and bake for 12 minutes. Remove from the oven and unroll the parchment packets, reserving the cooking liquid. Slide the fish onto individual serving plates. Pour the cooking liquid over the fish and serve immediately.

Serves 4

Brown Stew Fish and Fufu (Cornmeal with Okra)

Recipe from the kitchen of Verna Rose Martin

Serve this dish with watercress, lemon wedges, and tomato slices.

Brown Stew Fish

4 small whole red snappers, cleaned

4 small whole porgies, cleaned

1 cup lemon juice

2 teaspoons kosher salt

1 teaspoon freshly ground black
pepper

1 cup all-purpose flour

$^1/_4$ to $^1/_2$ cup vegetable oil

1 small onion, finely chopped

2 scallions, cut into $^1/_4$-inch-thick
pieces

3 garlic cloves, grated

1 medium tomato, cut into $^1/_4$-inch-
thick cubes

1 teaspoon cornstarch

2 teaspoons soy sauce

3 sprigs fresh thyme

Fufu

Two 13.5-ounce cans coconut milk

$^1/_2$ pound okra, trimmed and sliced
into $^1/_4$-inch rounds

1 large onion, chopped

1 teaspoon kosher salt

1 teaspoon freshly ground white
pepper

2 cups cornmeal

To prepare the Brown Stew Fish, wash the fish with cold water and lemon juice. Pat dry with paper towels. Season with the salt and black pepper. Place the flour in a shallow bowl and lightly coat the fish with it. Heat the oil in a large skillet over medium-high heat. Add the fish and fry for 2 to 3 minutes on each side. Transfer the fish to a large plate. You will need to fry the fish in batches, using up to $1/2$ cup oil as necessary. Add the onions, scallions, and garlic to the skillet and sauté until the vegetables soften. Add the tomatoes and continue to heat through. Combine the cornstarch with 1 tablespoon water in a small bowl and add to the skillet, followed by the soy sauce. Return the fish to the skillet, add the thyme, and simmer gently for 5 minutes, or until juices run clear when pierced.

To prepare the Fufu, place the coconut milk in a large saucepan over medium-high heat and bring to a boil. Add the okra, onion, salt, and pepper. Lower the heat and simmer for 3 minutes, or until the okra is partially cooked. Slowly add the cornmeal, stirring constantly with a wooden spoon to prevent lumps from forming. Add water, $1/4$ cup at a time, if the cornmeal mixture is too thick. Cover, reduce the heat to low, and simmer for 8 to 10 minutes. Spoon the Fufu into a large serving bowl. Place the fish stew on top and serve immediately.

Serves 4

Alabama Salmon

Recipe from the kitchen of Richard Clark

My mother used to make this dish, and it was the first recipe she taught me to make.

Food coloring is commonly being added to farm-raised salmon, so it's best to avoid it. Read the label if you're buying salmon from the grocery store, or if you're buying from a fish market be sure to ask if coloring has been added to the fish.

3 pounds salmon fillets
Juice from 4 lemons
1 small garlic clove
1 teaspoon ground ginger
$^{1}/_{2}$ teaspoon salt

$^{1}/_{4}$ teaspoon freshly ground black
   pepper
$^{1}/_{2}$ cup white cooking wine or
   Worcestershire sauce

Wash the salmon with the lemon juice and place in a large bowl. Place the garlic in a mortar and pestle, and crush it into a paste. Place in a small bowl and add the ginger, salt, pepper, and wine or Worcestershire sauce. Spread the mixture over the salmon fillets, cover with plastic, and set aside to marinate in the refrigerator for 1 to 3 hours. Place the salmon in a pressure cooker for 15 to 20 minutes. You can also steam the salmon on the stovetop by placing it in a steamer basket set over a pan of simmering water. Cook until fish flakes.

Serves 6 to 8

Richard Clark and son.

Sole Casserole

Recipe from the kitchen of Tara Posey

When my girlfriend Pam and I were in college, we were on a budget and didn't have a lot of time for cooking, so we would prepare this casserole almost every week.

This is a deliciously satisfying main dish with a variety of flavors coming together. Serve over brown rice.

$^3/_4$ cup carrots cut into $^1/_4$-inch-thick slices

Vegetable oil spray for the dish

Eight 6- to 8-ounce sole fillets

$^3/_4$ cup zucchini cut into $^1/_4$-inch-thick slices

1 medium green pepper, cored, seeded, and cut into $^1/_4$-inch-thick slices

2 large onions cut into $^1/_4$-inch-thick slices

$^1/_2$ pound Chinese pea pods, trimmed

$^1/_2$ pound white button mushrooms, cut into $^1/_4$-inch-thick slices

One 2.25-ounce can sliced black olives

4 tablespoons unsalted butter, cut into small pieces

1 tablespoon garlic powder

1 teaspoon cayenne pepper

2 tablespoons tamari sauce

$^1/_2$ cup shredded cheddar cheese

$^1/_2$ cup shredded Monterey Jack cheese

Salt

Freshly ground black pepper

Preheat the oven to 375°F.

Parboil the carrots in a small pot of boiling water and drain. Coat a large glass casserole with a cover of vegetable oil spray. Add the fish in a single layer and scatter the carrots, zucchini, green pepper, onions, pea pods, mushrooms, and olives over the fish. Dot with the butter. Add the garlic powder, cayenne, and tamari. Cover and bake for 25 minutes. Remove the cover and sprinkle the shredded cheeses over the top. Cover, return to the oven, and bake for 2 to 3 minutes longer, or until the cheeses melt. Remove from oven and season with salt and pepper to taste. Serve immediately.

Serves 8

Baked Fillet of Sole with Cheese

Recipe from the kitchen of Ms. Patricia Lelia Proctor, church trustee, and wife of former pastor Samuel DeWitt Proctor's son Herbert Proctor

This low-sodium dish is served with yellow rice and vegetables on the side.

4 tablespoons light, low-sodium margarine or vegetable oil spread

2 garlic cloves, chopped

2 basil leaves, chopped

Six 4-inch-long pieces fillet of sole

1 teaspoon Salt Sense

$^1/_4$ teaspoon freshly ground black pepper

Six $^1/_4$-inch-thick slices light, low-sodium cheddar cheese

2 scallions, chopped

Preheat the oven to 400°F.

Coat a large glass baking dish with the margarine and place in the oven until the margarine melts. Remove from the oven, add the garlic and basil, and stir until evenly distributed. Coat both sides of the fish pieces with the margarine mixture and place the fish in the baking dish. Sprinkle with the Salt Sense and pepper. Place a cheese slice on each piece of fish. Sprinkle the scallions over the fish. Cover the baking dish with foil and bake for 15 minutes. Remove the cover and bake for an additional 10 minutes, or until cheese melts. Serve immediately.

Serves 6

Sassy Salmon

Recipe from the kitchen of Yvonne M. Blackwell

I learned how to cook from my grandma Marion R. Williams by sitting on a high stool in her kitchen and watching her at work. My grandma was a wonderful cook, and she also was a sassy woman. As a Golden Age member (age eighty and over) of Abyssinian Baptist Church, grandma began attending back when the church was located on Waverly Place, before the move to its current location in Harlem.

When I was about sixteen years old, I began transporting grandma to Abyssinian in Harlem every Sunday. To motivate me to get up and take her, grandma used to make me homemade pancakes on the grill with sausage.

This recipe is my own creation, the first of several that I have come up with over the past year in my efforts to eat more healthful foods. I often think of my grandma when I make special dishes like this one, and I have named it Sassy Salmon in her honor.

Yvonne likes to say this prayer, from the Prayer of Jabez, King James Bible, Old Testament, to help expand and enlarge our healthful food territory: "Oh, that You would bless me indeed, and enlarge my territory, that Your hand would be with me, and that You would keep me from evil, that I may not cause pain."

$^1/_2$ teaspoon dried dill

$^1/_2$ teaspoon dried basil

2 garlic cloves, crushed

1 teaspoon sugar

4 salmon steaks, 4 to 6 ounces each

2 medium yellow onions, sliced into rings

2 tablespoons Italian salad dressing

2 tablespoons red wine vinegar

Combine the dill, basil, garlic, and sugar in a small bowl. Coat the salmon with the seasoning mixture, place in a large glass baking dish, and place the onions on top. Add the Italian dressing and red wine vinegar, cover with foil, and refrigerate for at least 4 hours, or overnight.

Preheat the oven to 350°F. Bake the salmon for 20 to 30 minutes with the foil on, or until firm to the touch.

Serves 4

Members of the congregation pose in front of the Abyssinian Baptist Church at Waverly Place, New York City, circa 1907.

Escoveitched Fish

*Recipe from the kitchen of the late
Manasseh Gordon*

Born in Jamaica, "Mr. G.," as he was affectionately called, migrated to England and
moved to the United States after he retired. He became a member of the
Abyssinian Baptist Church in 1985 where
he served as an usher and in the entertainment ministry until his death in 2005.

Manasseh Gordon.

1 pound red snapper or bluefish, split,
    with heads removed
1 teaspoon salt
$^1/_2$ teaspoon freshly ground black
    pepper
$^1/_4$ cup vegetable oil

1 large onion, sliced
1 Scotch bonnet chile, seeds and
    membrane removed, sliced
    $^1/_8$-inch thick
3 tablespoons white vinegar

Clean the fish and pat it dry. Season the fish with the salt and pepper. Heat the
oil in a large skillet over medium to high heat. Add the fish and fry until crisp,
about 5 minutes each side. Remove the fish to a platter. Add the onion and chile
to the skillet and sauté until translucent. Pour in the vinegar and cook another
minute. Spoon the onion mixture over the fried fish and serve.

Serves 4

Fish Stew

Recipe from the kitchen of Carole Darden-Lloyd

Our father loved all manner of seafood, and he particularly loved a good fish stew during the winter months. I think of him every time I prepare this dish.

1 pound cod fillet, cut into 1-inch
   cubes
2 dozen medium shrimp, shelled and
   deveined
2 large garlic cloves, crushed
4 tablespoons extra-virgin olive oil
1 large onion, chopped
2 medium red or yellow peppers,
   cored, seeded, and cut into $^1/_4$-inch
   strips and then into thirds

2 tablespoons tomato paste
Two 8-ounce bottles clam juice
Two 15-ounce cans diced tomatoes
1 teaspoon Italian seasoning
$^1/_2$ teaspoon red pepper flakes
   (optional)
$^2/_3$ cup white wine
Salt
Freshly ground black pepper

Toss the fish and the shrimp with the garlic in a medium bowl. Heat the oil in a large pot over medium heat. Add the onions and peppers and cook until softened and golden. Add the tomato paste and clam juice and stir until well blended. Stir in the tomatoes, Italian seasoning, red pepper flakes, if using, and the wine. Simmer for 10 minutes, then season with salt and pepper to taste. Add the fish and shrimp, bring to a simmer, and cook for 5 minutes, or until the fish is cooked through.

Serves 4

Pan-Seared Salmon Salad with Goat Cheese and Honey Vinaigrette

Recipe from the kitchen of Brian Washington-Palmer

My friend Toye Wigley has frequently complained that there aren't enough light, healthy dishes to eat in Harlem restaurants. Never mind that she was always trying to drag me out to I-Hop, where the plates are piled as big as my head. But she does love salmon, so I came up with something especially for her that would have the zing of syrup and the creaminess of butter. Not pancakes exactly, but two miles of biking a day and minus twenty pounds later, Toye is still eating the salmon salad, which she attributes to the new her. She looks fabulous, by the way, and eventually did get me to the famous International House of Pancakes. (I ordered a BLT...)

Honey Vinaigrette

1 cup rice vinegar

1 cup white balsamic vinegar

1^1/$_2$ cups orange juice

^{1}/$_4$ cup honey

^{1}/$_2$ cup olive oil

Salmon Salad

16 asparagus stalks

Four 6-ounce pieces salmon fillet,
   skin removed

Vegetable oil

Salt

Freshly ground black pepper

Dry herb rub (optional)

^{1}/$_2$ pound mesclun greens,
   (2^1/$_2$–3 cups)

2 Granny Smith apples, cored and
   sliced ^{1}/$_4$–inch thick

6 ounces goat cheese

To make the vinaigrette, combine the rice vinegar, balsamic vinegar, orange juice, and honey in a large bowl and whisk to dissolve the honey. Slowly add the oil, whisking constantly to combine. Set aside.

Bring a large pot of water to a boil, add the asparagus, and cook for 2 minutes—no more, or it will be soggy. Cut off the bottom part of the stalks and place the asparagus on a serving plate.

Lightly brush each piece of salmon with the oil. Sprinkle with salt and pepper to taste and rub the herb mix all over. Set a stovetop grill pan over high heat and let it get very hot. Place the salmon pieces on the grill and cook for about 3 minutes—you'll see the grill marks on the salmon. Turn and cook for another 3 minutes. Set aside.

Just before the salmon is ready, toss the mesclun with the vinaigrette in a large bowl and place over the asparagus. Decorate with the apple slices, and place the salmon pieces on top. Crumble the goat cheese over the salad.

Serves 4

Salmon Shaneon with Amaretto Sauce

Recipe from the kitchen of Teon and Shani Baker

Shani: I have been a member of Abyssinian since I was thirteen years old. Abyssinian has been a major part of my life—it's like family. My most memorable moment—of many at Abyssinian—was my wedding day.

My husband joined Abyssinian two years after we were married there. I can't tell you how happy I was to see him walk down the aisle that Sunday and give his life to God. And how happy his mother, Sheila, at rest with God, must have been.

Teon: My most memorable moments at Abyssinian are the day I married my wife and the day I got baptized. Tied for third place are the sermons delivered by Dr. Bill Cosby and Dr. Cornel West.

Shani: Teon and I love to cook together. He is more of a gourmet chef and I am more of a make-a-meal-out-of-anything type of gal. We often give each other a hard time in the kitchen, but it is fun and romantic. So with my Jamaican style and his Food-Network style, it works—like our marriage. One day we invited my mother, Fay Daley, over for dinner. We made up this recipe together that day on the phone before she came over.

The Amaretto Sauce should be prepared first because you'll need to use $^1/_4$ cup of the sauce for the stuffing. Serve with your favorite vegetables.

Amaretto Sauce

2 tablespoons unsalted butter

$^3/_4$ cup evaporated milk

$^1/_4$ cup Amaretto

Pinch of sea salt

$^1/_4$ teaspoon ground nutmeg

$^1/_4$ teaspoon ground cinnamon

1 teaspoon cornstarch

1 tablespoon sugar

Salmon

3 tablespoons olive oil

Four 7-ounce fillets salmon, cut down the center to create a pocket for stuffing

Salt or Bragg Liquid Aminos

Freshly ground black pepper

2 teaspoons fresh or dried thyme

One 6-ounce box cornbread stuffing mix

1 large red onion, finely chopped

2 garlic cloves, chopped

$^1/_2$ pound large shrimp, peeled, deveined, and cut in half lengthwise

2 tablespoons sugar

$^1/_4$ cup Amaretto sauce (see Headnote)

To prepare the Amaretto sauce, melt the butter in a medium skillet over medium heat. Add the evaporated milk, Amaretto, salt, nutmeg, and cinnamon and bring to a simmer. Cook, stirring, for 3 to 4 minutes. Remove from the heat and set aside. Remove $^1/_4$ cup of the sauce at this point to use with the stuffing. Combine $^1/_3$ cup water with the cornstarch in a small bowl and stir until well blended. Add to the Amaretto sauce and return to the heat. Add the sugar and simmer, stirring until the sauce thickens. Set aside.

Preheat the oven to 375°F. Grease a large baking pan with 1 tablespoon of the oil and set aside. Season the salmon with salt or Bragg Liquid Aminos, pepper, and thyme and set aside on a large plate. Prepare the stuffing according to the directions on the box. Heat the remaining 2 tablespoons oil in a medium sauté pan. Add the onion and garlic and sauté until they begin to soften. Add the shrimp and sauté for 3 to 4 minutes, or until pink. Do not overcook the shrimp.

Add the shrimp to the stuffing mix, then add the sugar and a pinch of salt. Cool, then add the reserved $1/4$ cup Amaretto sauce to the stuffing. Gently and generously stuff the salmon with the stuffing, but do not overstuff. Place the salmon skin side down in the oiled baking pan. Dip 4 long toothpicks or skewers in oil and stick them through the ends of the salmon to hold the fish and stuffing together. You can put the leftover stuffing in the pan around the salmon. Bake uncovered for 30 minutes, or until the fish flakes easily with a fork. Remove the fish from the pan with a spatula. If it doesn't stick, remove the skin from the fish. Place the salmon on serving plates and top with the Amaretto sauce.

Serves 4

Big Ferg's Tuna-Mac Salad

Recipe from the kitchen of Reverend Darren A. Ferguson

When I was about twelve years old, my mother underwent a full hysterectomy. I was an only child, so it was my responsibility to care for her during her recovery. I prepared meals for her, making sure that there was something easy for Mom to fix for lunch while I was at school. One Sunday night, I got in the kitchen and started boiling macaroni, separating the tuna, and adding every spice that I could from our pantry to make it taste good. Being a kid and having a tremendous sweet tooth, I added sweet relish as an afterthought because I wanted the finished product to be sweet. My mother loved the salad, even though we ate it every day for dinner for a week. God bless her soul, she was even more patient, because she had to eat it for breakfast and lunch! Ever since, I have been asked to bring some Big Ferg's Tuna-Mac Salad to every family function. My daughter even requests it to take to fellowships at her school.

Seasoned Salt, Adobo, or other all-in-one seasonings can be used in this dish—it should be seasoned to your particular taste. If you like spicy food, you can add cayenne, Tabasco sauce, or anything else that excites your taste buds. Including diced radishes or carrots adds taste, crunch, and color to this dish.

The amount of mayonnaise can be either increased or decreased to your taste. Whatever the consistency, the dish will firm up with refrigeration. Those who are weight-conscious can substitute low-carb or lite mayonnaise if desired.

1½ pounds cooked macaroni

Two 6½-ounce cans tuna (preferably albacore)

½ large green pepper, cored, seeded, and diced

½ large red pepper, cored, seeded, and diced

½ large red onion, diced

1 celery rib, diced

¾ cup sweet relish

1½ cups mayonnaise

4 tablespoons hot mustard

Freshly ground black pepper or cayenne pepper, to taste

Garlic powder, to taste

Lawry's Seasoned Salt, or other seasoned salt, or adobo, to taste

Paprika, for garnish

4 large hard-boiled eggs, 3 chopped, 1 sliced

Combine all the ingredients except the paprika and sliced egg in a large bowl. Sprinkle lightly with paprika and decorate the top with the sliced egg. Refrigerate for 2 hours before serving. Serve over a bed of lettuce or baby spinach.

Serves 6

Rev. Darren Ferguson and his wife, Kim Ferguson.

Rice and Beans

BILL BOYD

Rice Pilaf

Recipe from the kitchen of Verna Rose Martin

This recipe calls for kosher or sea salt, which draw out the flavors in a dish, and are among the purest salts available. It also calls for long-grain rice, which cooks nicely into separate grains.

2 tablespoons unsalted butter	$^1/_2$ cup white wine
1 medium onion, chopped	$3^1/_2$ cups chicken stock
2 cups long-grain rice	1 teaspoon kosher or sea salt
1 bay leaf	$^1/_2$ teaspoon ground white pepper

Melt the butter in a small saucepan with a tight-fitting lid over medium heat. Add the onion, cover the lid, and sweat the onion for 1 minute. Remove the lid and add the rice, bay leaf, wine, stock, salt, and pepper. Cover and bring to a boil. Reduce the heat to medium-low and simmer for 20 minutes, or until rice is done and water absorbed.

Serves 6 to 8

Cuban Black Beans in a New York Minute

Recipe from the kitchen of Ms. Dolores Simanca

This is my signature Cuban-Caribbean dish. I learned how to cook black beans from my mother, who always made them on Sundays. When I was growing up in Spanish Harlem during the 1950s and '60s, cooking and eating black beans was unique to Cubans and Cuban Americans. Not anymore!

This recipe has been adapted to substitute canned beans for fresh, which makes for shorter preparation time. The beans can be served as a side dish or soup.

One 16-ounce can black beans
$^1/_2$ cup low-sodium or salt-free
   chicken stock
1 teaspoon ground cumin
$^1/_4$ teaspoon ground coriander

$^1/_4$ teaspoon freshly ground black
   pepper
1 large garlic clove, crushed
1 bay leaf
1 tablespoon olive oil

Combine the beans, stock, cumin, coriander, pepper, and garlic in a medium saucepan over medium heat. Bring to a simmer, lower the heat, add the bay leaf and oil, and cook until desired consistency. Serve over white or yellow rice.

Variation: To make black beans and rice, omit the bay leaf and increase the olive oil to $^1/_4$ cup. Add 1 cup uncooked white rice and enough chicken stock to cover by 1 inch. Stir, cover, bring to a simmer, lower the heat, and cook for 10 to 12 minutes, or until the liquid is absorbed.

Serves 4 to 6

Rice and Peas

Recipe from the kitchen of the late Manasseh Gordon

2 cups dried pigeon peas or red
  kidney beans
  or one 15-ounce can
1 fresh coconut or one 13.5-ounce can
  coconut milk

Thyme
Salt
$2^1/_4$ cups rice

If dried peas are being used, presoak for 2 to 3 hours in a bowl with water to cover by 2 inches.

If using a fresh coconut, break and remove the coconut from the shell and peel off the brown husk. Grate the coconut or cut it into small pieces and grate it in a food processor. Squeeze the coconut over a strainer and reserve the coconut milk.

Combine the peas, thyme, salt to taste, and coconut milk in a medium saucepan over high heat and bring to a boil. Lower the heat and simmer for 20 to 30 minutes, or until peas mash when gently pressed with a wooden spoon, but are not mushy. Add the rice and 3 cups water. Bring to a boil, cover, then lower the heat and cook for 10 to 12 minutes, or until the liquid is absorbed.

Serves 4 to 6

Yellow Rice with Green Peppers and Pigeon Peas

Recipe from the kitchen of the late Manasseh Gordon

The rice also can be prepared without the pigeon peas and served with Cuban Black Beans (see recipe page 144).

1 pound (4 cups) yellow rice
    (available in Hispanic or Caribbean
    markets)
1 large green pepper, cored, seeded,
    and diced

One 14-ounce can pigeon peas,
    drained
1 tablespoon unsalted butter

Bring 3 cups water to a boil in a large pot. Add the rice, cover the pot, lower the heat, and simmer until the rice is half cooked. Add the green pepper, peas, and butter. Stir, then cover and simmer for 30 minutes, or until all the liquid is absorbed.

Serves 4 to 6

Southern Black-Eyed Pea Croquettes

Recipe from the kitchen of Walter E. Clark

2 cups day-old cooked black-eyed
   peas
1 large egg, beaten
$^1/_2$ medium onion, diced
Pinch of baking powder

Salt
Pepper
$^1/_4$ cup milk
$^1/_4$ cup vegetable oil, plus more as
   needed

Place the peas in a large bowl and mash them to a paste. Add the egg, onion, baking powder, salt and pepper to taste, and milk. Shape the mixture into balls and flatten them. Heat the oil in a large skillet over medium-high heat. Add the patties to the skillet and fry 4 to 5 minutes each side, or until crisp and browned. Remove to a large plate. Add more oil as needed and fry until all the croquettes have been made.

Makes 8 to 10 croquettes

Pasta

Macaroni and Cheese (page 154).

Amy Ruth's Shrimp Lasagna

Recipe from the kitchen of Mr. Carl S. Redding, proprietor of Amy Ruth's

Amy Ruth's restaurant has been a Harlem eatery treasure since 1998. It is named for proprietor Carl Redding's grandmother Amy Ruth Moore Bass, a devout Christian woman from whom he learned to appreciate the culinary arts. His mother, Inez Bass, sent her children to spend the summer months in the South. It was, says Redding, "somewhat safer than the big city of New York. During those summer months, each one of my brothers, Eric and Gregory, and my two first cousins, Ahmed and Marten, were assigned various tasks. The main tasks included mowing the rather large lawn and picking various vegetables in the garden. Not liking the hot sun, I would seek refuge in the house with my grandmother, who would be hard at work preparing breakfast, supper, and dinner. I would always find my way to my grandmother's side, helping her prepare those meals under her direction. If I wasn't shucking the many ears of corn, I would be peeling field peas, or rolling out the biscuit dough with a broomstick." Those summer experiences caused Redding's love for Southern cuisine to grow and led him to open a restaurant specializing in it. His style varies widely, however, as proved by this simply delicious lasagna.

9 cooked lasagna noodles

4 tablespoons unsalted butter, softened

1 medium onion, chopped

$^2/_3$ cup all-purpose flour

2 cups half-and-half

2 cups dry white wine

2 pounds medium shrimp, peeled, deveined, and cut into $^1/_2$-inch pieces

1 pound sharp cheddar cheese, shredded

Salt

Freshly ground black pepper

$^1/_2$ cup heavy cream

Chopped fresh parsley

Preheat the oven to 350°F.

Lightly grease a 12-inch shallow ovenproof dish. Add a layer of lasagna sheets, filling in all gaps. Set aside. Melt the butter in a large saucepan over low heat. Add the onion and cook until translucent. Stir in the flour and cook for 1 minute, or until the mixture starts to foam. Remove from the heat and gradually stir in the half-and-half and wine. Place over medium heat and cook, stirring constantly, until the sauce starts to boil and thicken. Reduce the heat and simmer for 2 minutes. Add the shrimp and simmer for 1 minute, or until shrimp just turn pink. Remove the skillet from the heat. Stir in three quarters of the cheese and salt and pepper to taste. Spread half of the shrimp mixture over the lasagna sheets and cover with another layer of lasagna sheets. Spread the remaining shrimp mixture over the lasagna sheets and cover with a final layer of lasagna sheets. Pour the cream on top and sprinkle with the shredded cheese and parsley. Bake uncovered for 30 minutes, or until bubbling and golden brown.

Serves 6

Tricolor Pasta with Spinach and Plum Tomatoes

Dr. Anita Underwood.

Recipe from the kitchen of Dr. Anita Underwood

My first corporate job was overseas. I ate well there without gaining any weight. I discovered there were two reasons for this: preservatives and portion control. There are profound differences in the way Americans and Europeans process food. And the portions in European restaurants are small and meals are served in courses, so it takes longer to eat your meal. Meals should be slow, long, and conversational; you chew your food well and give it time to digest. Contrast that with what we do in the States: we're served very large portions and we eat very quickly. Your body can't break down food properly when you scoff it down.

I've been a vegetarian since 1975, and I am now in 2005 moving toward a diet that includes more raw or live plant foods. I get more nutrients out of what I eat when the natural enzymes are still in them. Cooking and processing destroy the natural enzymes. When I say raw, a frown usually spreads across people's faces. They think of raw broccoli, raw cauliflower, and no taste. Raw or live means it's not cooked over 118 degrees. Using a thermometer, I heat distilled water to 116 degrees. I put broccoli, for example, in the water and in a flash the temperature drops. The broccoli is bright green, a bit less al dente, and very flavorful, yet still retains its live enzymes. For protein I sometimes use edamame, raw soybeans that look like pea pods. I buy them frozen so they thaw out quickly in the 116 degree water, and it becomes a complete protein snack. Drinking almond milk is another way to get your protein in a live food diet. You use it in the same way that you would use regular milk.

Many people have added more vegetables to their diets, but when you cook vegetables you're only getting 20 percent of the enzymes, so you're mostly just getting fiber. My foray into live foods is similar to what it was like being a vegetarian thirty years ago—we're a small group, and people think that what we eat is strange and un-appetizing—but I find it quite interesting and exciting. My ultimate goal is for my diet to be comprised of 60 percent live foods and 40 percent cooked. Vegetarian dishes like this are a rare treat for me.

One 16-ounce package tricolor
   pasta
1 tablespoon olive oil
1 large red onion, chopped finely
3 garlic cloves, chopped finely
2 celery ribs, chopped 1/4-inch thick

1 cup fresh spinach, chopped into
   1/2-inch pieces
2 plum tomatoes, chopped into
   1/4-inch pieces
1 teaspoon sea salt
1/4 teaspoon cayenne pepper

Cook the pasta according to the package directions, drain, and set aside. Heat the oil in a large sauté pan over high heat. Add the onion, garlic, celery, and spinach and sauté until the vegetables soften. Add the pasta, followed by the tomatoes. Toss to coat the pasta. Add the salt and cayenne and toss. Serve hot or cold.

Serves 4 to 6

Sun-Dried Tomato and Black Olive Alfredo with Grilled Shrimp

BILL BOYD

Recipe from the kitchen of Kenneth Rasul

The shrimp can be sautéed in the marinade if a grill is not available.

One 16-ounce package penne pasta
2 teaspoons chopped fresh thyme
   leaves
2 teaspoons chopped fresh oregano

3 garlic cloves, finely chopped
$^1/_2$ cup olive oil
24 jumbo shrimp, peeled and
   deveined

Alfredo Sauce

1 quart heavy cream
$^1/_2$ cup sun-dried tomatoes packed in
   oil, drained and julienned
$^1/_2$ cup sliced black olives
Salt

Freshly ground black pepper
$1^1/_4$ cups grated Parmesan cheese
2 tablespoons unsalted butter
$^1/_4$ cup diced fresh chives
1 large tomato, seeded and diced

Cook the pasta according to the package directions, drain, and set aside.

Combine the thyme, oregano, garlic, and oil in a large bowl. Add the shrimp and toss to coat. Preheat a grill, remove the shrimp from the marinade, and cook until the shrimp turns pink. Set aside.

To make the alfredo sauce, heat the heavy cream in a large saucepan over medium-high heat until it thickens slightly. Add the sun-dried tomatoes, olives, and salt and pepper to taste. Fold in the pasta, then add 1 cup of the Parmesan and the butter. Garnish with the chives, fresh tomato, and the remaining $^1/_4$ cup Parmesan. Top with the shrimp.

Serves 6

Baked Shrimp Parmesan Pasta

Recipe from the kitchen of Student Recipe Testers

1 pound penne pasta

2 tablespoons olive oil

1¹/₂ pounds jumbo shrimp, peeled,
   deveined, and tails removed

1 large onion, chopped

1 garlic clove, chopped

One 28-ounce can tomato sauce

One 14¹/₂-ounce can diced tomatoes

1 teaspoon kosher salt

¹/₂ teaspoon freshly ground black
   pepper

1 tablespoon Italian seasoning

¹/₄ cup grated Parmesan cheese

One 8-ounce package mozzarella
   cheese, shredded

Preheat the oven to 350°F.

Prepare the pasta according to the package directions, drain, and set aside. Heat 1 tablespoon of the oil in a large skillet over medium-high heat. Add the shrimp and sauté until pink on both sides, 4 to 5 minutes. Remove the shrimp to a platter. Heat the remaining 1 tablespoon oil in a large saucepan with a lid over medium heat. Add the onion and garlic and sauté until translucent, about 1 to 2 minutes. Add the tomato sauce, diced tomatoes, salt, pepper, Italian seasoning, and 2 tablespoons of the Parmesan. Bring to a boil, then reduce the heat, cover, and simmer for 35 minutes, or until heated thoroughly and flavors are well blended. Create layers in the following order: Spoon ¹/₂ cup sauce in the bottom of a large baking dish, then add the pasta followed by 1 cup of the sauce, then the shrimp, and finally another 1 cup sauce. Sprinkle the mozzarella and the remaining 2 tablespoons Parmesan on top. Cover with foil and bake for 35 to 40 minutes, or until the cheese melts. Remove the foil and bake 5 minutes longer, or until the cheese starts to brown. Serve with the remaining sauce passed at the table.

Serves 4 to 6

Macaroni and Cheese

Recipe from the kitchen of Bernice Parks

4 cups dried #2 ziti

10 ounces extra-sharp cheddar
cheese, shredded

One 12-ounce can evaporated milk

2 large eggs

1 teaspoon onion powder

1 teaspoon garlic powder

1 teaspoon Sylvia's Lemon Pepper
Seasoning

2 teaspoons Sylvia's Seasoned Salt

1 teaspoon Cajun seasoning

$1/4$ teaspoon ground nutmeg

1 tablespoon Dijon mustard

2 tablespoons I Can't Believe It's Not
Butter, cut into small chunks

1 cup breadcrumbs, optional

2 teaspoons paprika

Preheat the oven to 350°F.

Cook the ziti according to the package directions and set aside.

Spread a layer of ziti over an 8-inch square baking pan. Follow with a layer of cheese. Repeat the layering, ending with a layer of cheese.

Whisk together the evaporated milk, eggs, onion powder, garlic powder, lemon pepper seasoning, seasoned salt, Cajun seasoning, nutmeg, and mustard in a medium bowl. Pour the mixture over the macaroni and cheese. Evenly distribute the butter substitute chunks on top. Sprinkle with the breadcrumbs and paprika. Cover with foil and bake for 50 minutes, or until a knife inserted comes out clean. Remove the foil and bake 5 minutes longer, or until golden brown.

Serves 4

Vegetable and Meat-Free Dishes

Stovetop Eggplant Parmesan (page 166).

Sautéed Spinach

Recipe from the kitchen of Verna Rose Martin

One 10-ounce package fresh spinach

4 tablespoons unsalted butter

1 large onion, chopped

$^1/_2$ teaspoon kosher salt

$^1/_4$ teaspoon ground white pepper

$^1/_8$ teaspoon ground nutmeg

Wash the spinach thoroughly in enough water to remove any lingering dirt or sand. Heat the butter in a medium skillet over medium heat. Add the onion, cover, and cook until translucent. Add the spinach and cook for 3 minutes, stirring constantly. Season with the salt, white pepper, and nutmeg.

Serves 2

Caribbean Yuca

Recipe from the kitchen of Ms. Dolores Simanca

Dolores Simanca.

Native to South America, yuca became an important staple of Africa after the transatlantic slave trade. Yuca is a root vegetable akin to the potato and makes an interesting side dish as a change from pasta or potatoes. It has a crisp white flesh and tough brown skin, which can be difficult to peel. Always scrub the yuca clean and peel off all of the skin, or you can buy frozen yuca, which is already peeled.

1 pound yuca, peeled	1 large garlic clove, chopped
$^1/_4$ cup olive oil	1 lime

Bring a medium pot of water to a boil and boil the yuca until a fork can go through it easily. It should have the same consistency as a boiled white potato. Drain into a colander, cool slightly, and slice. Heat the oil in a large skillet over medium-high heat. Add the garlic and sauté until translucent, about 1 minute. Add the yuca to the skillet and stir to thoroughly coat the yuca with the oil and garlic. Remove to a platter and squeeze lime juice on top while the dish is still steaming hot, just before serving. The whole dish will sizzle!

Variation: Just boil the yuca, drain, and sprinkle with salt and pepper.

Serves 4 to 6

Sweet Potato Soufflé

Recipe from the kitchen of Bess N. Reynolds

I was blessed to have a mother who was a wonderful cook, and the smells coming from her kitchen early on a Sunday morning were enough to wake anyone up with a big grin. Whenever she made my favorite, sweet potato soufflé, I would sit at the kitchen table in deep silence and with great anticipation as she combined all the ingredients in her favorite green mixing bowl. I was always allowed to help pour the batter into the baking dish and given the spoon afterward to lick.

6 medium sweet potatoes

$^1/_2$ cup (1 stick) unsalted butter

$^1/_4$ cup milk

1 cup sugar

1 teaspoon ground cinnamon

1 teaspoon ground nutmeg

1 cup mini marshmallows

Preheat the oven to 325°F.

Place the sweet potatoes in a large pot of water, bring to a boil, and simmer for 15 to 20 minutes, or until tender. Drain the sweet potatoes and peel them as soon as they're cool enough to handle. Return the sweet potatoes to the pot while still warm and mash with a potato masher. Add the butter and milk, then stir in the sugar, cinnamon, and nutmeg. Fold in the marshmallows. Transfer to a 2-quart baking dish and bake for 30 minutes, or until firm.

Serves 4 to 6

Veggie Chili

Recipe from the kitchen of Ms. Shirley V. Corbino

Serve this healthy and hearty chili as a main dish.

1 medium onion, finely diced

1 garlic clove, minced

6 ounces meatless ground "beef" crumbles

1 cup frozen corn, thawed

1 small zucchini, diced

One 8-ounce can tomatoes with green chiles, with juices

One 27-ounce can pinto beans, rinsed and drained

One 1.75-ounce envelope chili seasoning mix

Combine all the ingredients in a large pot over medium-high heat. Stir well and bring to a boil. Reduce the heat to medium and simmer, uncovered, for 30 minutes, or until heated throughout, stirring frequently to prevent sticking.

Serves 4 to 6

Sautéed Kale

Recipe from the kitchen of Tara Posey

This is a fast and healthy way to prepare these nutrient-rich leafy greens without using smoked meats. I remember my local grocer used to use kale mostly as a decoration back when I was a child, so I thought it wasn't to be eaten. We enjoyed collards, mustard greens, and turnips in my family, and I later learned to love kale.

2 tablespoons extra-virgin olive oil
1 large white onion, quartered and
   sliced
$^1/_2$ medium red pepper, cored, seeded,
   and thinly sliced
2 garlic cloves, crushed

1 bunch kale, rinsed, stems removed,
   and coarsely chopped
$^1/_4$ cup chicken stock
1 tablespoon hot pepper vinegar
Salt
Freshly ground black pepper

Heat the oil in a large saucepan over medium heat. Add the onion, red pepper, and garlic and sauté 3 to 4 minutes, or until soft. Add the kale and sauté 2 to 3 minutes, or until wilted. Add the stock and vinegar, stir, and reduce the heat to low. Cover and simmer until the kale is tender, 15 to 20 minutes. Add salt and pepper to taste.

Serves 4

Stovetop Eggplant Parmesan

Recipe from the kitchen of Dr. Anita Underwood

1 medium eggplant, peeled and cut into $^1/_2$-inch-thick slices

1 teaspoon sea salt

$^1/_2$ teaspoon cayenne pepper

$^1/_4$ cup plus 2 tablespoons extra-virgin olive oil

1 cup spicy Italian breadcrumbs

One 8-ounce package part-skim mozzarella cheese, shredded

One 16- or 17-ounce jar tomato sauce with basil, heated

2 tablespoons chopped fresh basil

$^1/_2$ cup freshly grated Parmesan cheese

Sprinkle the eggplant slices with salt and cayenne and brush both sides of the eggplant slices with $^1/_4$ cup of the oil. Place the breadcrumbs in a shallow bowl and coat the eggplant with the breadcrumbs. Heat the remaining 2 tablespoons oil in a large skillet over medium-high heat. Add the eggplant and cook until tender, about 3 minutes. Sprinkle the mozzarella over the eggplant, cover the pan, and cook until the cheese is melted. Spread half of the tomato sauce on top, sprinkle with the basil and Parmesan, and top with the rest of the tomato sauce.

Serves 4

BILL BOYD

Succotash

Recipe from the kitchen of Carole Darden-Lloyd

Succotash has its origins with American Indian cuisine. But it certainly found its way into my culinary roots with consistency during the summer months when fresh vegetables were plentiful. All my aunts cooked it, but no recipe was exactly the same. This is my version, combined from many sources.

6 slices turkey bacon

$^1/_2$ tablespoon extra-virgin olive oil

1 small onion, sliced

2 garlic cloves, minced

8 ounces baby pattypan squash, trimmed and quartered

Kernels from 4 ears corn, cobs scraped to extract their juice

One 10-ounce package frozen baby lima beans or soybeans, thawed

1 large jalapeño chile, seeded and finely chopped

$^1/_2$ pound okra, trimmed and cut into rounds

1 pint cherry tomatoes, halved

2 tablespoons cider vinegar

$^1/_4$ cup chopped fresh basil

Salt

Freshly ground black pepper

Cook the bacon in a large skillet over medium-high heat until crisp on both sides. Place on paper towels to drain. Add the oil to the same skillet, reduce the heat to medium, add the onion, and cook until golden. Add the garlic and cook for 1 minute, or until soft. Add the squash, corn, lima beans, jalapeño, and okra. Increase the heat to medium-high and cook, stirring, until the vegetables are just tender, about 8 minutes. Add the tomatoes, vinegar, basil, and salt and pepper to taste and heat through. Crumble the bacon on top.

Serves 8

Zucchini Fritters

Recipe from the kitchen of
Dotsie Gore

Dotsie Gore, mother of Bob Gore, chairman of the
Trustee Board at Abyssinian.

4 medium zucchini

2 cups all-purpose flour

2 teaspoons salt

1 teaspoon baking powder

2 medium eggs, beaten

1 cup milk

1 tablespoon grated onion

$1^1/2$ cups peanut oil

Trim the zucchini but do not peel. Grate the zucchini into a colander and drain for 30 minutes. Wrap the zucchini in a towel to absorb excess moisture. Combine the flour, salt, and baking powder in a large bowl. Add the eggs, milk, and onion and stir until smooth. Add the zucchini to the batter. Place the oil in a large skillet over high heat. Drop the batter by spoonfuls into the oil. Fry the fritters, turning once, until golden brown on both sides, about 5 minutes total. Remove the fritters from the oil and drain on paper towels. Repeat with the remaining batter to finish the fritters.

Makes 30 fritters, serves 6 to 8

Meatless Greens

Recipe from the kitchen of Carole Darden-Lloyd

When I was a child, our home was never without a large yellow Pyrex bowl of greens in the refrigerator. They were cooked in a huge pot with one ham hock for seasoning. They would last through the week, and the ritual was repeated the following weekend. We didn't know then, as the following recipe proves, that you could lose the ham hock and still love the greens.

3 tablespoons extra-virgin olive oil

1 large yellow onion, sliced

$^1/_2$ teaspoon red pepper flakes
   (optional)

$^1/_2$ cup cider vinegar

Salt

Freshly ground black pepper

6 pounds collard greens or any
   combination of greens, such as
   mustard, kale, or turnip, tough
   stalks removed and torn into
   coarse pieces

Heat the oil in a large pot over medium-high heat. Add the onion and cook until the onion begins to brown, about 2 to 3 minutes. Lower the heat, cover, and cook for 20 to 25 minutes, or until the onions are softened and thoroughly browned. Stir frequently to prevent burning. Add 6 cups water, the red pepper flakes, if using, the vinegar, and salt and pepper to taste. Raise the heat, bring to a boil, and add the greens. Lower the heat to medium-low and cook, partially covered, stirring occasionally, for 20 to 25 minutes, until the greens are tender but not soft.

Serves 8 to 10

Tofu Loaf

Recipe from the kitchen of Fay Daley

Fay Daley.

When I was in high school in Jamaica, West Indies, I considered myself fat. After I graduated, I wanted to lose weight, so I started researching cleansing diets. As a result, I began to eat more fruits and fiber and stopped eating fried foods. I started losing weight, which got me more interested in eating right.

God had a purpose for this change that went beyond my personal appearance because years later I would use this information to create a church-wide Lenten fast.

To drain and press tofu, put the block of tofu between two towels and place a weight on top, or sit the tofu on a strainer over the sink, cover with a towel, and place a weight on top. Let drain for at least 20 minutes. Bragg Liquid Aminos can be found in health food stores.

4 slices pumpernickel bread

Two 16-ounce packages firm tofu,
   drained and pressed

1 scallion, chopped

1/2 small onion, chopped

1/2 teaspoon fresh thyme leaves

cherry tomatoes, halved

2 tablespoons chopped red pepper

1 cup blanched and chopped
   broccoli

1/2 teaspoon cayenne pepper

2 tablespoons Bragg Liquid Aminos

1 large egg, beaten

1/4 cup breadcrumbs

1 teaspoon paprika

1 teaspoon chopped fresh parsley

Preheat the oven to 350°F.

Soak the bread in a medium bowl filled with water. Drain the excess water. Crumble the tofu and bread together and place in a large bowl. Add the scallion, onion, thyme, tomatoes, red pepper, broccoli, cayenne, and Bragg. Stir in the egg and mix well. Place the tofu in a 9-inch loaf dish or pan. Sprinkle the bread-crumbs and paprika on top. Bake for 30 minutes, or until firm and heated through. Garnish with the parsley.

Serves 6 to 8

BILL BOYD

Vegetarian Zucchini Tomato Casserole

Recipe from the kitchen of Suzanne Woodard

My father, who was very concerned about his diet, and my husband, Reverend Dino Woodard, who is a vegetarian, inspired my healthier take on this dish, which I first came across in Baltimore more than fifteen years ago. This low-fat vegetarian version has become a family favorite.

2 large zucchini, cut into $^1/_4$-inch slices

2 yellow squash, cut into $^1/_4$-inch slices

1 medium onion, diced

1 package powdered vegetable broth

1 teaspoon sugar

One 14.5-ounce can stewed tomatoes

$^1/_3$ cup jarred spaghetti sauce

Preheat the oven to 350°F.

Place the zucchini, yellow squash, onion, vegetable broth, and sugar in a medium casserole. Toss. Add $^1/_3$ cup water, cover the dish, and bake for about 20 minutes, or until vegetables are not quite tender. Remove from the oven and pour off the excess liquid. Add the stewed tomatoes and spaghetti sauce and stir well. Return to the oven and bake until the vegetables are tender, about 10 minutes.

Serves 4

Seasoned Cabbage

Recipe from the kitchen of Reverend Kevin R. Johnson

This recipe is from my wife's grandmother, Armateen Pendleton Howard, whom everyone called Grandma Teen. My wife, Kimya Pendleton Johnson, and I learned how to make this recipe from her during our first Christmas as a married couple, in December 1997. We were living in New York City and didn't have much money, so we decided to visit Grandma Teen, who lived in Birmingham, Alabama, during the holidays, since going to her house was like staying in a wonderful bed and breakfast. I am so glad we made the trip because it was the last time we saw her alive; she died in September 1998.

Watching Grandma Teen make cabbage was far from my first experience in the kitchen. My mother Dorothy Nell Johnson and my grandmother Sedalia Johnson taught me how to cook. They were great cooks. Sundays always meant a big home-cooked meal in our house and Thanksgiving, Christmas, and the first Sunday of the New Year, when Reverend James E. Obey Sr., the pastor of my home church, David Chapel Missionary Baptist, would come by, were feasts for which they would prepare for weeks ahead.

I would watch the whole holiday preparation. My mother was a big cake person—she was always cooking something new. Her 7-Up Cake was a big hit, and she would always make a gourmet presentation.

My grandmother stuck to the cooking traditions, like "chitlins" (chitterlings), which she only made once a year—for New Year's Sunday. She started cleaning them during the last days of November and she'd freeze them. She would clean the greens at least two weeks before, and she would make the pies the week before. They sat, covered, where I could see them but not touch them. I would watch her make the crust for her peach cobbler. She'd roll the dough, put it into a huge rectangular lasagna pan, pour in her cooked peaches, lay in the second layer of dough, pour in more juicy peaches, and then put on that final layer of dough. She'd carefully make the edges with a wet fork and sprinkle the sugar, cinnamon, and nutmeg on top.

Grandma would cook all through the night, waking up at various hours to go and stir her greens. It reminded me of feeding a newborn baby.

I could tell Christmas was getting closer by the delicious aromas that filled the house.

When I made that newlywed trip to visit Grandma Teen, I could still make pie crust from scratch. But I had not cooked cabbage before, and despite growing up in a household of fabulous cooks, I had never tasted cabbage made like this. My grandmother made cabbage, but Kimya's grandmother prepared it in a way I had never seen, tearing the leaves off the head, rolling them up, and cutting them into strips.

Kimya and I created this recipe over the years, which is a combination of both of our families' recipes, and the bouillon was added by Kimya.

1 large head white cabbage
4 slices fatback or bacon
1 small chicken bouillon cube

1/8 teaspoon Lawry's Seasoning Salt or
    other seasoned salt
1 teaspoon freshly ground black pepper

Tear the leaves off the head of cabbage and wash them 3 times. Roll up the leaves and cut them into 3-inch-wide strips. Place the fatback in a large pot over medium heat and cook until crisp. Place the cabbage on top of the meat. Do not add any water.

Grate the bouillon onto the cabbage, add the Lawry's Seasoning Salt and pepper to taste, and cook until tender, but not too soft, 15 to 20 minutes, stirring every ten minutes.

Serves 4 to 6

Southern Fried Corn

Recipe from the kitchen of Willie Moore and Dorothy Burns

3 cups young, tender, fresh white corn
    kernels cut from the cob

$^1/_2$ teaspoon salt

$^1/_4$ teaspoon freshly ground black
    pepper

$^1/_4$ cup self-rising flour

3 slices bacon

Combine the corn, salt, pepper, $^1/_2$ cup water, and flour in a mixing bowl. Fry the bacon in a medium skillet over medium-high heat, turning once, until crisp, about 2 minutes. Remove the bacon from the skillet and drain on paper towels, but leave the drippings. Add the corn mixture to the skillet, cover, reduce the heat to medium, and cook the corn for about 8 minutes, until it starts to soften, stirring frequently. Remove from the heat and serve immediately.

Variation: For a thicker consistency, combine $^1/_4$ cup of water with the flour in a cup and blend well. Add the flour mixture to the corn when it's done cooking. Reduce the heat and simmer, stirring constantly, 2 to 3 minutes longer, or until desired consistency.

Serves 4

Salads

Cold Black-Eyed Pea Salad (page 186).

Toni's Salad with Honey Mustard Dressing

Recipe from the kitchen of Carole Darden-Lloyd

4 cups mesclun or any variety of baby greens and lettuce

1/4 cup coarsely chopped cilantro

1/2 small red onion, thinly sliced

3 large radishes, thinly sliced

1 medium carrot, thinly sliced

2 medium yellow peppers, cored, seeded, cut in half, and sliced 1/4-inch thick

1 1/2 boneless, skinless chicken breasts, halved, then grilled and cut in 1/2-inch strips

2 tablespoons dried cranberries

1/2 cup halved cherry tomatoes

1/4 cup black beans, rinsed and drained

1/2 ripe avocado, coarsely chopped

1/4 cup unsalted sunflower seeds, briefly toasted in a dry skillet

Honey Mustard Dressing

1/4 cup red wine vinegar

3/4 cup extra-virgin olive oil

2 tablespoons Dijon mustard

1 garlic clove, crushed

1 teaspoon Vegesal

1 1/2 tablespoons honey

To make the salad, combine the greens and cilantro in a large salad bowl. Add the remaining ingredients in the order given. Toni considers this an artistic blend of color, texture, and flavor, so personal preference is encouraged. Do not toss.

To make the Honey Mustard Dressing, place all the ingredients in a blender or food processor and blend for 1 minute. You can also place all the ingredients in a jar with a lid and shake well to combine. However, the dressing will be completely emulsified by the blender method and will retain a superior consistency.

To serve, dip salad tongs deep into the bowl so that each serving will contain all of the layered ingredients, and divide among serving plates. Drizzle the Honey Mustard Dressing over each serving.

Serves 4 to 6

Bulgur Salad

Recipe from the kitchen of Verna Rose Martin

This is a completely satisfying meat-free meal and a great summer dish. This recipe comes from the school of live, or raw foods—what Verna refers to as "sun-fried" cooking. It's nutritious, high in fiber, low in calories and cholesterol, quick to prepare, and colorful and tasty. You'll find bulgur (cracked wheat) at health food stores.

Bulgur Salad

2 cups bulgur (cracked wheat)

1 large tomato, cut into $1/4$-inch-thick cubes

2 scallions, sliced $1/4$-inch thick

1 tablespoon soy sauce

2 teaspoons ground cumin

1 avocado, peeled and sliced $1/4$-inch thick

Alfalfa sprouts (optional)

1 teaspoon tahini (sesame paste)

1 teaspoon West Indian hot pepper sauce

Salad Topping

1 small green cabbage, finely shredded

2 carrots, sliced $1/4$-inch thick

2 beets, peeled and sliced $1/4$-inch thick

1 bunch radishes, sliced $1/4$-inch thick

4 pieces okra, trimmed and sliced $1/4$-inch thick

Dressing

$1/3$ cup fresh lemon juice

$1/2$ teaspoon kosher salt

1 teaspoon freshly ground black pepper

3 garlic cloves, grated

1 cup olive oil

To prepare the salad, place the bulgur in a large bowl with 2 cups cold water. Add the tomatoes, scallions, soy sauce, and cumin and stir to combine. Let sit 4 to 6 hours, or overnight, in refrigerator. The bulgur will soften and double in volume.

To prepare the salad topping, place all the salad vegetables in a medium bowl and toss.

To prepare the dressing, combine the lemon juice, salt, pepper, and garlic in a medium bowl. Slowly add the oil, whisking, until thoroughly combined, or combine the ingredients in a jar with a lid and shake vigorously. Place equal portions of the bulgur salad on serving plates. Decoratively arrange the salad topping on top, placing the avocado slices and alfalfa sprouts in the center. Drizzle the dressing on top, followed by the tahini and hot sauce, if using.

Serves 4

Potato Salad

Recipe from the kitchen of Zana Billue, recipe tester

Everyone talks about how great my mother's potato salad is. Once I took it to school for a holiday party and left it in the teachers' cafeteria until the party started. A couple of hours later one of the teachers pulled me out of class to tell me she had taken some of the potato salad for her lunch, and that it was delicious.

The secret to keeping the potatoes firm is to boil them the day before you prepare the potato salad.

3 pounds (6 to 8) red potatoes

2 large hard-boiled eggs, chopped

1 medium onion, chopped fine

1 green or red pepper, cored, seeded, and chopped

1 celery rib, chopped

1 cup mayonnaise

$^1/_2$ cup Miracle Whip salad dressing

$^1/_2$ cup sweet relish

2 teaspoons seasoned salt

1 teaspoon kosher salt or celery salt

$^1/_2$ teaspoon sugar

$^1/_4$ teaspoon ground nutmeg

1 teaspoon freshly ground black pepper

Place the potatoes with their skins on in a large pot with just enough water to cover and bring to a boil over high heat. Reduce the heat and simmer until tender. Remove from the heat. Place the potatoes in a large bowl, cover with plastic, and place in the refrigerator to cool. Peel the potatoes and cut them into 1-inch cubes. Place the potatoes back in the bowl. Add the eggs, onions, green or red pepper, celery, mayonnaise, salad dressing, and relish. Stir until well combined. Add the seasoned salt and kosher salt, sugar, nutmeg, and black pepper. Mix again until the seasonings are well distributed. Cover with plastic and refrigerate for at least 2 hours before serving.

Serves 6 to 8

Coleslaw

Lee Dunham

Recipe from the kitchen of Lee Dunham

1 medium white cabbage, tough outer
   leaves removed and finely
   shredded
1 medium carrot, shaved with a
   vegetable peeler
$^1/_2$ red pepper, cored, seeded, and
   diced
$^1/_2$ yellow pepper, cored, seeded, and
   diced
$^1/_2$ green pepper, cored, seeded, and
   diced
6 radishes, thinly sliced
4 small tomatoes, halved and seeds
   removed
1 cucumber, halved and seeds
   scooped out, then quartered and
   thinly sliced

4 scallions, trimmed and finely
   chopped
2-inch piece ginger, peeled and finely
   chopped
4 heaping tablespoons sweet pickle
   relish
$^3/_4$ cup mayonnaise, or to taste
1 teaspoon garlic powder
Salt
Freshly ground black pepper

Combine all the vegetables in a large bowl. In a small bowl, combine the ginger,
pickle relish, mayonnaise, garlic powder, and salt and pepper to taste. Pour the
dressing over the vegetables and toss to coat. Cover with plastic and refrigerate
for at least 2 hours to allow the flavors to blend together well. Serve chilled or at
room temperature.

Serves 6 to 8

Avocado Salad

Recipe from the kitchen of Ms. Dolores Simanca

1 small head of Romaine lettuce

2 medium tomatoes, quartered

1 small red onion, thinly sliced

1 avocado, peeled, pitted, and sliced

1 cup pitted black olives, sliced

$^{1}/_{2}$ olive oil

$^{1}/_{4}$ cup fresh lemon juice

Combine the lettuce, tomatoes, onion, avocado, and olives in a large bowl. Add the oil and lemon juice and toss.

Serves 2 to 3

Cold Black-Eyed Pea Salad

Recipe from the kitchen of Mrs. Robbye McMillan

$^1/_2$ cup parboiled rice

One 10-ounce package frozen baby
    lima beans

Three 16-ounce cans black-eyed peas

1 medium red pepper, cored, seeded,
    and diced

3 tablespoons chopped fresh parsley

2 tablespoons lemon juice

2 tablespoons vegetable oil

1 tablespoon Dijon mustard

1 teaspoon sugar

$^3/_4$ teaspoon salt

Prepare the rice and lima beans according to the package directions. Rinse and drain the black-eyed peas. In a large bowl, combine the pepper, parsley, lemon juice, oil, mustard, sugar, and salt. Add the rice, lima beans, and black-eyed peas and stir to combine. Cover with plastic and refrigerate for 1 hour before serving.

Serves 4 to 6

Breads

BILL BOYD

Broccoli Cheese Cornbread (page 199).

Corn Sticks

Recipe from the kitchen of Ms. Shirley V. Corbino

If you bake the corn sticks ahead of time, wait to slice them until ready to serve.

1 cup fine yellow cornmeal

1 cup all-purpose flour

2 tablespoons sugar

1 tablespoon baking powder

1 teaspoon salt

1 large egg

1 cup milk or buttermilk

$^1/_2$ cup (1 stick) unsalted butter, melted

Preheat the oven to 425°F.

Grease an 8-inch baking pan and set aside. Combine the cornmeal, flour, sugar, baking powder, and salt in a large bowl. Stir in the egg, milk or buttermilk, and butter. Beat for 1 to 2 minutes, or until smooth. Pour the batter into the pan and bake for 15 to 20 minutes, or until golden brown. Remove from the pan, cut into 1 by 4-inch strips and serve hot.

Serves 6

Waffles Plus Six

Recipe from the kitchen of Ms. Betty Anne Syphrette

This healthy waffle recipe is made with six wholesome grains and can be served for breakfast topped with pineapple, blueberries, or blackberries, or as a main dish with chicken or fish cakes.

1 cup whole wheat flour	4 teaspoons baking powder
2 ounces ($^1/_4$ cup) cornmeal	$^1/_2$ teaspoon salt
2 ounces ($^1/_4$ cup) bulgur	4 large eggs, separated
2 ounces ($^1/_4$ cup) barley	1 cup skim milk
2 ounces ($^1/_4$ cup) kasha	5 tablespoons unsalted butter, melted
2 ounces ($^1/_4$ cup) oats or wheat germ	4 tablespoons sugar

Preheat the waffle iron.

Combine the whole wheat flour, cornmeal, bulgur, barley, kasha, oats or wheat germ, baking powder, and salt in a large bowl. Beat the egg yolks with the milk and butter in a separate large bowl. Add the egg mixture to the flour mixture and stir until smooth. Beat the egg whites and sugar in another bowl until soft peaks form. Fold the egg whites into the batter using a rubber spatula. Do not overmix. Oil the waffle iron and spread $^1/_2$ cup of the batter onto the waffle iron and cook according to the manufacturer's instructions. Repeat with the rest of the batter. Garnish the waffles with your choice of berries.

Makes 4 to 5

Golden Brown Corn Pancakes

Recipe from the kitchen of Eva B. Frazer Jordan

1 cup fine cornmeal	1 large egg
1 teaspoon baking powder	2 tablespoons milk (more if you like
$\frac{1}{2}$ teaspoon salt	the consistency of pancakes thinner)
$\frac{1}{2}$ teaspoon sugar	4 tablespoons vegetable oil
	Honey or butter

Sift the cornmeal into a large bowl. Add the baking powder, salt, and sugar and stir to combine. Whisk the egg with the milk in a small bowl. Add the egg mixture to the cornmeal mixture and beat well. Heat 1 tablespoon of the oil in a small saucepan over medium heat. Add the hot oil to the batter. Beat well into a workable consistency. Heat the remaining 3 tablespoons of oil in a medium skillet over medium heat. Pour $\frac{1}{4}$ cup of the batter into the skillet. Cook until lightly browned and bubbles appear on the edges, then flip and cook until lightly browned on the other side. Remove to a platter and continue cooking pancakes until all the batter has been used. Serve with honey or butter.

Serves 3 to 4

Soft Gingerbread

Recipe from the kitchen of Bessie M. Nixon

I was born and raised on a farm in Georgia. We had everything on that farm—horses, cows, pigs, and chickens. We milked the cows, put the milk in enameled bowls, and let the cream rise to the top. We then skimmed the cream off and put it in a churn to make butter. The milk that was left from the butter was called "butter milk." My mother would make this delicious gingerbread and we would have a good time eating it hot, slathered with the butter we had churned, and drinking cool buttermilk.

2^1/$_2$ cups all-purpose flour

^{1}/$_2$ cup sugar

1 teaspoon grated fresh ginger

1 teaspoon ground cloves

1 teaspoon ground cinnamon

2 teaspoons baking soda

1 cup boiling water

^{1}/$_2$ cup unsalted butter, melted, or
    vegetable oil

1 cup molasses

2 large eggs, beaten

Preheat the oven to 350°F. Grease an 8-inch square baking pan and set aside.

Combine the flour, sugar, ginger, cloves, and cinnamon in a large bowl. Combine the baking soda, boiling water, butter, and molasses in a medium bowl. Add the wet ingredients to the flour mixture and mix well. Add the eggs and mix again. Pour the mixture into the baking pan and bake for 40 to 45 minutes, or until test knife or skewer comes out clean.

Let cool for 15 to 20 minutes before cutting.

Serves 6 to 8

Sweet Potato Biscuits

Recipe from the kitchen of Ruth E. Willis

My mom, Ruth E. Willis, recently turned eighty-two. I am amazed at what a close-knit family we still have. She is the oldest of five sisters. I used to marvel at them when I was a child, listening to them talking and laughing about growing up during the Depression and sharing eventful stories of survival and *foodways*. Two of my most distinctive memories include the making of sweet potato biscuits and homemade wine (see page 245). I used to squint my face and ask, "Why make sweet potato biscuits and wine?"

My mom replied, "Mom Foreman always wanted to make her meals exciting, and she liked variety with her Sunday meals, especially when she made a roast pork and fried chicken." My mom's grandmother, Catherine Foreman, known to us as Mom Foreman, taught her how to make the biscuits from leftover sweet potatoes. I was seven years old when Mom Foreman died at the age of seventy-seven. Born in 1880 in Elizabeth City, North Carolina, she was the family matriarch. Her husband, Edward Foreman, served in the Spanish-American War and later worked as a brick mason and on the Erie Lackawanna railroad. After her death, stories upon stories were told to us, her grandchildren and great grandchildren, and those stories all involved food.

$^1/_2$ pound cooked and mashed sweet
   potatoes
$^1/_2$ cup (1 stick) margarine or unsalted
   butter, softened
$^2/_3$ cup milk

$^1/_4$ cup honey
$1^1/_2$ cups all-purpose flour
1 tablespoon baking powder
$^1/_2$ teaspoon salt

Preheat the oven to 400°F.

Combine the sweet potatoes, margarine or butter, milk, and honey in a large bowl. Combine the flour, baking powder, and salt in a medium bowl. Add the dry ingredients to the sweet potato mixture and mix until the dough forms a ball. Place the dough on a floured surface and roll and press the dough to a $1/2$-inch-thick rectangle. Cut into rounds using a biscuit cutter or drinking glass. Place on an ungreased sheet pan with the sides touching. Bake for 15 to 20 minutes, or until edges begin to brown.

Makes 2 dozen

Broccoli Cheese Cornbread

Recipe from the kitchen of Myrna Sanders

I was born and raised in Florida in a family of ten children. With ten kids my father grew everything and raised pigs and chickens. We also had a smokehouse where he made sausage. All of us kids had to learn to cook. We did things together as a family because with so many children my mother and father just told us what we had to do, and we did it. We are still a tight-knit group. That's probably why we're so guarded about our family recipes. Initially I wasn't going to release any family secrets!

I'll never forget what happened the first time I baked a pie. I must've been fourteen years old. My mom went to church one day and left me instructions: "The pie is already done. All you have to do is roll the crust out, put it in the pan, and put the filling in." So I rolled out the crust, but it was crooked. So I put more flour on it, rolled it back up, and rolled it out a second time. Even though it was still crooked I went on and baked it anyway. When I took it out of the oven it was hard as a rock. My mother came home and asked me what happened. I explained to her that after I rolled out the dough the first time, it was crooked, so I rolled it out again. Right away she knew the problem. "You didn't keep putting flour on it, did you?" she asked. I replied, "Yes ma'am, I did." It's funny that my first attempt at baking turned out that way, especially when you consider that as an adult I once made two hundred pies in one week here at Abyssinian when the Brotherhood (a male ministry engaged in prayer and study to support the pastor and various church activities) had a pie sale for Thanksgiving.

My first experience cooking outside my family was at Lord & Taylor, where I worked in new accounts as a customer service supervisor. Since I was head of the department I obviously wanted my people to get out the applications. I found that I could get my entire staff of twelve to stay late if I made them lunch. We usually got behind during the holiday season when we would process as many as thirty thousand new accounts a month. To bring in some variety, I started looking at cookbooks and testing out new recipes. At this point I have at least fifty cookbooks, and my collection is still growing.

Because I'm in the kitchen all day on Sunday (see page 16), I seldom get to go to church, except during the summer when the kitchen closes for the month of August. People are usually shocked when they find out I'm not a member of Abyssinian because I've been here so many years. I'm a member of Canaan Baptist Church of Christ, but I feel like I belong here. Sometimes I miss Canaan, but the people of Abyssinian have taken me into their arms. After I had my two rotator cuffs replaced in 1997 so many people from Abyssinian, even some that I didn't know, called me to see how I was doing. I was really shocked. I enjoy being here and I enjoy what I do. I especially enjoy the older people, helping them out and seeing them enjoy the food. It has crossed my mind to join Abyssinian because it really is like a family here. And this cornbread recipe is one of the most popular among my Abyssinian family!

One 7- to 8-ounce box corn muffin mix

1 cup sour cream

3 large eggs, beaten

One 10-ounce box frozen chopped
    broccoli

1 cup shredded sharp cheddar cheese

$^1/_2$ large onion, chopped

$^1/_2$ cup (1 stick) unsalted butter or
    margarine, melted and cooled

1 teaspoon salt (optional)

Preheat the oven to 375°F. Generously grease a 9-inch skillet or pie pan and set aside.

Combine the corn muffin mix, sour cream, and eggs in a large bowl. Add the broccoli, cheese, onion, butter and salt, if using, and mix until well blended. Pour the batter into the prepared pan. Bake for 25 minutes, or until the bread is golden brown and springs back when touched.

Variation: Add 1 cup corn kernels or $^1/_2$ cup chopped red pepper to the batter.

Serves 6 to 8

Banana Bran Muffins

Recipe from the kitchen of Carole Darden-Lloyd

A hot muffin for breakfast is a wonderful comfort food. These muffins are simple to prepare and their healthful ingredients make them a perfect substitute for the additive-filled store-bought variety.

1 large egg

$^1/_2$ cup light brown sugar

1$^1/_3$ cups mashed ripe bananas

$^1/_2$ cup chopped walnuts

$^1/_3$ cup canola oil

1 teaspoon vanilla extract

$^3/_4$ cup unbleached all-purpose white
    flour

$^3/_4$ cup whole wheat flour

$^1/_2$ cup oat bran

2 teaspoons baking powder

$^1/_2$ teaspoon baking soda

1 teaspoon ground cinnamon

Preheat the oven to 375°F. Grease a standard 12-muffin tin and set aside.

Lightly beat the egg in a medium bowl. Add the brown sugar, mashed banana, walnuts, oil, and vanilla and stir until well blended. Sift together the flours, oat bran, baking powder, baking soda, and cinnamon into a large bowl. Add the banana mixture and stir until moistened but not smooth. Divide the batter among the muffin tins, filling them two-thirds full. Bake for 15 to 20 minutes, or until golden and firm to the touch.

Makes 10 to 12 muffins

Banana Bread

Recipe from the kitchen of Jo-Ann Garner and Brunetta Garner

Originally from Ellisville, Mississippi, Joe Garner joined Abyssinian in 1981, and four years later married Tramel, who had been a member of the Church since childhood and whose father had served on the deacon board. Their son Jared Garner was born in 1991.

The entire family—both the New York and the Mississippi branches and all the living generations—is "partial to good cooking." The Garner recipes came from family members and friends from the Gulf Coast—his mother, Brunetta Garner, his sister Jo-Ann Garner, and his niece Tramel McMillan; and from Walter and Tommie Jean Clark, family friends that make up their New York contingent of cooks.

$^1/_3$ cup vegetable shortening	1 teaspoon vanilla extract
$^1/_2$ cup sugar	2 cups all-purpose flour
2 large eggs	1 teaspoon baking soda
$^1/_4$ cup buttermilk	$^1/_2$ teaspoon salt
1 cup mashed ripe bananas	$^1/_2$ cup chopped walnuts

Preheat the oven to 350°F. Grease a 9-inch loaf pan and set aside.

Cream together the shortening, sugar, eggs, buttermilk, bananas, and vanilla. Sift the flour, baking soda, and salt into a medium bowl and add to the egg mixture. Mix well. Fold in the walnuts. Pour the batter into the pan and bake for 50 to 60 minutes, or until firm to the touch.

Serves 4 to 6

Zucchini Bread

Recipe from the kitchen of Carole Darden-Lloyd

Our parents always kept a vegetable garden while we were growing up. In the later years zucchini became a particular favorite, but no matter how little one planted, there always seemed to be more squash than one could actually eat. Zucchini Bread became a tasty solution. Drain the zucchini in paper towels after shredding it to remove excess water.

3 cups unbleached all-purpose flour
1 teaspoon baking powder
$^3/_4$ teaspoon baking soda
1 teaspoon salt
1 teaspoon ground cinnamon
$^1/_2$ teaspoon ground nutmeg
3 medium eggs

1 cup canola oil
$1^1/_2$ cups raw sugar
1 teaspoon vanilla extract
1 cup chopped walnuts
1 cup raisins
1 pound zucchini, ends removed,
    unpeeled and shredded

Preheat the oven to 350°F. Grease a tube or two 9-inch loaf pans and set aside.

Combine the flour, baking powder, baking soda, salt, cinnamon, and nutmeg in a large bowl. Beat the eggs in a medium bowl. Add the oil, sugar, and vanilla and mix well. Pour the egg mixture into the flour mixture. Add the walnuts, raisins, and zucchini and mix well. Pour the batter into the prepared pan(s) and bake for 1 hour, or until a toothpick inserted in the center comes out clean. Let cool 15 minutes in pan, then remove from the pan to a wire rack to cool completely.

Serves 8 to 10

BILL BOYD

Dinner Rolls

Recipe from the kitchen of Felicia Gray

These rolls are a favorite at our family dinners. They melt in your mouth, especially when they're fresh out of the oven. You cannot eat just one! And they are especially good the next day with sliced baked ham.

1 cup milk

$^1/_2$ cup sugar

2 packages active dry yeast

4 cups all-purpose flour

1 teaspoon salt

$^1/_2$ cup vegetable shortening

2 large eggs, beaten

Scald the milk in a small saucepan over medium-high heat. Transfer to a medium bowl. Stir in the sugar and cool to lukewarm, 105° to 110°F. Add the yeast and stir until the yeast dissolves. Combine the flour and salt in a large bowl. Cut in the shortening until small beads form. Create a well in the flour mixture, add the eggs and milk mixture, and stir until the dough is moist. Turn the dough out onto a lightly floured surface and knead until smooth, about 5 minutes. Place in a large oiled bowl and cover with a damp kitchen towel. Let rise for 1$^1/_2$ to 2 hours, or until nearly doubled in bulk. Punch down. Grease a large baking sheet and set aside. Place on a lightly floured surface and roll the dough out until it is $^1/_4$ inch thick. Cut into circles using a biscuit cutter or drinking glass. Fold each circle in half. Place the rolls side by side on the baking pan.

Preheat the oven to 350°F.

Cover the rolls with plastic wrap and let rise for 40 to 60 minutes, or until doubled in bulk. Remove the plastic wrap and bake for 20 minutes, or until golden brown. Serve hot.

Makes 2 dozen

Whipping Cream Biscuits

Recipe from the kitchen of Dorothy Nell Johnson, mother of Reverend Kevin R. Johnson

2 cups self-rising flour, plus some for dusting

1 tablespoon sugar

$1^1/_2$ cups heavy whipping cream

Preheat the oven to 500°F. Grease a large baking sheet and set aside.

Combine the flour and sugar in a medium bowl. Add the cream and stir until the dough forms a ball. Turn the dough out onto a lightly floured surface. Fold the dough in half and knead 5 to 7 times, adding just enough flour to keep the dough from sticking to your hands. Gently roll out the dough to a $^1/_2$-inch-thick rectangle. Cut the dough into circles using a 3-inch biscuit cutter coated with flour. Place on the baking sheet, leaving at least 1 inch between each biscuit. Bake for 10 minutes, or until golden brown. Serve immediately.

Makes $1^1/_2$ dozen biscuits

Desserts

Apple Pound Cake (page 222).

Sweet Potato Pudding

Recipe from the kitchen of the late Manasseh Gordon

2 pounds (4 to 8) peeled and grated
    sweet potatoes
1 cup coconut milk
1 tablespoon vanilla extract
1 tablespoon ground allspice

1 tablespoon freshly ground nutmeg
1 cup all-purpose flour
2 cups brown sugar
$1/2$ pound raisins

Preheat the oven to 350°F. Grease a 9 by 12-inch baking pan and set aside.

    Combine the sweet potatoes, coconut milk, vanilla, allspice, nutmeg, flour, brown sugar, and raisins in a large bowl. Pour the mixture into the baking pan and bake 1 hour and 30 minutes to 2 hours, or until mixture is firm.

Serves 8

Student recipe tester.

Apple Crumble with Vanilla Sauce

Recipe from the kitchen of Verna Rose Martin

This treat is like the English version of American apple pie, but much easier to prepare. It's inexpensive to make, and your children will love it.

Filling

1 pound Granny Smith apples, peeled, cored, and sliced $^1/_4$-inch thick

$^1/_3$ cup sugar

5 cloves, ground into a powder

Topping

1$^1/_2$ cups unbleached all-purpose flour

6 tablespoons margarine or unsalted butter, softened and cut into pieces

$^1/_3$ cup sugar

Vanilla Sauce

3 cups cow's milk or plain soymilk

5 teaspoons cornstarch

$^1/_2$ teaspoon vanilla extract

3 tablespoons brown sugar

Preheat the oven to 350°F.

To prepare the filling, combine the apples with the sugar and cloves in a large bowl. Transfer the mixture to a pie dish or deep ovenproof dish.

To prepare the topping, place the flour in a medium bowl and crumble the margarine or butter into the flour with your fingers to form small crumbs. Stir in the sugar. Spread the mixture on top of the apples and gently press down. Bake for 30 minutes, or until the topping is browned and the apples are tender.

Meanwhile, prepare the vanilla sauce: bring the milk just to a boil in a small deep saucepan over medium-low heat. Remove from heat. Combine the cornstarch with 1 tablespoon cold water in a small bowl and stir to dissolve until it is a smooth paste. Add the cornstarch to the hot milk, return to heat, stirring constantly to prevent lumps from forming, 5 to 6 minutes, or until thickened. Add the vanilla and brown sugar and pour over the warm apple crumble.

Serves 4

Silken Gingerbread

Recipe from the kitchen of Ms. Betty Anne Syphrette

My grandfather from Norfolk, Virginia, Grandfather King, often would bake this silken gingerbread for us on weekdays and serve it with hot cocoa. We would just sit there looking at each other, smiling and laughing and waiting for the bread to come out of the oven.

3 cups all-purpose flour

$^1/_2$ cup whole wheat flour

$1^1/_2$ teaspoons baking soda

$2^1/_2$ teaspoons ground cinnamon

2 teaspoons ground ginger

1 teaspoon ground allspice

1 teaspoon ground cloves

$^1/_2$ teaspoon ground nutmeg

$^1/_2$ cup (1 stick) unsalted butter, at room temperature

1 cup granulated sugar

$^1/_2$ cup brown sugar

3 large eggs

1 cup light molasses

$1^1/_2$ cups sour cream or buttermilk

Preheat the oven to 350°F. Grease a 13 by 9 by 3-inch baking pan and set aside.

Sift the flours, baking soda, cinnamon, ginger, allspice, cloves, and nutmeg together into a large bowl. Set aside. Cream the butter and granulated and brown sugars in a separate large bowl until fluffy. Add the eggs one at a time to the butter and sugar mixture, mixing after each addition. Combine the molasses with $^1/_4$ cup boiling water in a small bowl. Gradually add the molasses to the butter mixture and mix well. Slowly fold the dry ingredients into the butter mixture using a rubber spatula. Then slowly fold in the sour cream. Pour the batter into the baking pan and bake for 30 to 35 minutes, or until a toothpick inserted in the center comes out clean. Let cool in the pan on a rack for 10 minutes, then invert the cake onto the rack, allowing the gingerbread to cool right side up.

Serves 12

White Potato Pie

Recipe from the kitchen of Winona A. Green

My mother, Marie LaFrances Green, made this unique and tasty white potato pie while I was growing up in Baltimore.

7 medium potatoes	1 teaspoon ground nutmeg
½ cup (1 stick) unsalted butter	1 tablespoon vanilla extract
2 cups sugar	One 9-inch unbaked frozen piecrust
4 large eggs	

Preheat the oven to 350°F.

Place the unpeeled potatoes in a large pot with water to cover over high heat. Bring to a boil, lower the heat, and cook until the potatoes are soft. Peel the potatoes, place them in a large bowl, add the butter, and mash the potatoes. Add the sugar, eggs, nutmeg, and vanilla and mix with a hand-held electric mixer until smooth. Pour the mixture into the piecrust and bake for 1 hour, or until golden brown on top.

Makes one 9-inch pie, serves 8

BILL BOYD

White Potato Pie and Oscilla Sweet Potato Pie.

Ocilla Sweet Potato Pie

Recipe from the kitchen of Karen Phillips

My hometown, Ocilla, Georgia, considers itself the sweet potato capital of the world. I was Ocilla's first African American Grand Marshall at the 2001 annual Ocilla Sweet Potato Festival, and this is my family's recipe.

3 medium sweet potatoes, cooked
    and peeled while still warm
$^1/_2$ cup (1 stick) unsalted butter, at
    room temperature
1 cup granulated sugar
$^1/_4$ cup brown sugar

2 large eggs
1 teaspoon vanilla extract
1 teaspoon ground cinnamon
$^1/_2$ teaspoon ground nutmeg
$^1/_2$ teaspoon ground allspice
One 9-inch unbaked frozen piecrust

Preheat the oven to 350°F.

Place the sweet potatoes in the large bowl of an electric mixer while still warm and mash well at low speed. Add the butter and mix well. Add the granulated sugar, brown sugar, eggs, vanilla, cinnamon, nutmeg, and allspice and mix until well incorporated. Pour the mixture into the pie crust and bake for 50 to 60 minutes, or until set and lightly browned on top.

Makes one 9-inch pie

Karen Phillips at the 2001 Ocilla Sweet Potato Festival.

Mama Georgia's Sweet Potato Banana Pie

Recipe from the kitchen of Georgia Gowan

This custard pie never fails. It's from my grandmother, Mama Georgia, who absolutely loved to cook and was an excellent baker back in the days before electric mixers.

2 large eggs, separated

1 cup sugar

$^1/_2$ teaspoon ground cinnamon

$^1/_2$ teaspoon ground allspice

$^1/_2$ teaspoon ground nutmeg

3 medium sweet potatoes, cooked, peeled, and mashed

1 cup heavy cream

$^1/_2$ cup (1 stick) unsalted butter, melted

$^1/_4$ cup mashed ripe banana

One 9-inch unbaked frozen piecrust

Jason Curry, Thanksgiving Day Dinner Volunteer, 1994.

Preheat the oven to 450°F.

Place the egg yolks in the large bowl of an electric mixer and whip until thick. Add the sugar, cinnamon, allspice, and nutmeg and mix until the sugar dissolves. Add the sweet potatoes, cream, and melted butter and mix well. Add the banana, if using, and mix. In a separate bowl, beat the egg whites until stiff peaks form. Fold the egg whites into the sweet potato mixture and pour into the piecrust. Bake for 10 minutes, then reduce the oven temperature to 350°F and bake for 30 minutes longer, or until a toothpick inserted in the center comes out clean.

Makes one 9-inch pie

English Trifle

Recipe from the kitchen of Charlotte Page Scarborough

1 package ladyfingers or 1 pound cake,
   cut into 2-inch-thick pieces
1 cup sherry or rum (optional)
1 package Bird's English Custard Mix
4 cups milk
One 20-ounce can sweetened
   pineapple chunks, drained

3 or 4 bananas, cut into $1/4$-inch-thick
   slices
2 cups fresh or frozen strawberries
   halved (leave 4 or 5 whole for
   garnish)
1 cup heavy cream, whipped, or
   8 ounces Cool Whip

If using the rum, place the ladyfingers in a large bowl and pour the rum over them. Cover with plastic and soak the ladyfingers overnight. Prepare the custard according to the package directions, using all the milk. Let cool. Combine the pineapple, sliced bananas, and strawberries in a large bowl. Arrange the ingredients in layers, starting with half of the ladyfingers placed on the bottom and around the sides of a large glass serving bowl, followed by half of the custard, then half of the fruit. Repeat the layers with the remaining ingredients. Cover with whipped cream. Garnish with the whole strawberries. Keep refrigerated until ready to serve.

Serves 12

German Chocolate Cake with Coconut-Pecan Filling and Frosting

Recipe from the kitchen of Ms. E. Juanita McCray

I couldn't wait to try out this German Chocolate Cake recipe on my husband when I was a new bride. I followed the instructions carefully, prepared everything accordingly, and followed each step meticulously. I felt quite proud of myself as I put the pans of batter into the preheated oven set at the precise temperature. As the cake baked, I made the icing and placed a wire cooling rack in the center of my kitchen table with the icing close by. I placed the first layer on the rack, iced it, and did the same with the second and third layers. When I was finished I looked at the master-piece I had just created and smiled, and my masterpiece slowly sank right through the wire cooling rack and ended flat on the kitchen table. I could not move the cake or take out the rack without destroying this beautiful cake. For the rest of the week, until the cake was all gone, it sat front and center on the kitchen table. Now every time I make this cake, my husband says, "Remember the cooling rack is not part of the ingredients."

4 ounces chopped Baker's German's
    Sweet Chocolate
2 cups all-purpose flour
1 teaspoon baking soda
$1/4$ teaspoon salt
1 cup (2 sticks) unsalted butter,
    softened
2 cups sugar
4 large eggs, separated
1 teaspoon vanilla extract
1 cup buttermilk

Frosting

One 12-ounce can evaporated milk
$1^1/2$ cups sugar
$3/4$ cup ($1^1/2$ sticks) unsalted butter or
    margarine
4 large egg yolks, lightly beaten
$1^1/2$ teaspoons vanilla extract
One 7-ounce package Baker's Angel
    Flake Coconut (about $2^2/3$ cups)
$1^1/2$ cups chopped pecans

Line the bottoms of three 9-inch round cake pans with wax paper. Place the chocolate in a small microwaveable bowl with $^1/_2$ cup water and microwave on high for $1^1/_2$ minutes, or until the chocolate is almost melted, stirring halfway through. Stir until the chocolate is completely melted and set aside to cool. Combine the flour, baking soda, and salt in a large bowl. Beat the butter and sugar in the large bowl of an electric mixer on medium speed until light and fluffy. Add the egg yolks, one at a time, beating well after each addition. Stir in the melted chocolate and vanilla. Add the flour mixture alternately with the buttermilk, beating after each addition until smooth. Beat the egg whites in another large bowl with the electric mixer on high speed until stiff peaks form. Gently fold into the batter. Pour the batter into the prepared pans and bake for 30 minutes, or until the cake springs back when lightly touched in the center. Immediately run a spatula between the cake layers and sides of the pans. Cool for 15 minutes, then invert onto wire racks and remove the wax paper. Cool completely before frosting.

To make the frosting: Combine the evaporated milk, sugar, butter, egg yolks, and vanilla in a large saucepan over medium heat. Cook, stirring, for 12 minutes, or until thickened and golden. Remove from the heat. Add the coconut and pecans and stir until cool and of spreading consistency.

Spread the frosting between layers, on the sides, and over the top of the cake.

Variation: To melt the chocolate on the stovetop instead of the microwave, place the chocolate and $^1/_2$ cup water in a heavy one-quart saucepan over very low heat and heat, stirring constantly, until the chocolate is melted and the mixture is smooth. Remove from the heat to cool.

Serves 12

Apple Pound Cake

Recipe from the kitchen of Myrna Sanders

1 cup vegetable oil

4 large eggs

2 cups plus 2 tablespoons sugar

2 1/2 teaspoons vanilla extract

3 cups all-purpose flour

1 tablespoon baking powder

1/2 teaspoon salt

1/4 cup orange juice

2 large Granny Smith apples, peeled,
   cored, and thinly sliced

2 tablespoons ground cinnamon

1/4 teaspoon ground allspice

Powdered sugar, for sprinkling

Preheat the oven to 350°F. Grease and flour a 10-inch fluted cake pan and set aside.

Combine the oil, eggs, 2 cups of the sugar, and vanilla in a large bowl and beat until well mixed. In another large bowl, combine the flour, baking powder, and salt. Slowly add the flour mixture, alternating with the orange juice, to the egg mixture. Mix until well incorporated. In a large bowl, toss the apples, remaining 2 tablespoons sugar, the cinnamon, and allspice until the apples are well coated.

Spoon half of the batter into the prepared pan and top with half of the apples. Repeat with the remaining batter and apples. Bake until the top of the cake is lightly browned and firm to the touch, about 1 hour and 15 minutes. Cool the cake in the pan for about an hour, then remove the cake from the pan and sprinkle with powdered sugar.

Serves 10

BILL BOYD

Blueberry Salad

Recipe from the kitchen of D. D. King

My mother would make this at Thanksgiving or Christmas.

Salad

Two 3-ounce packages grape Jell-O

One 20-ounce can sweetened
  crushed pineapple, undrained

One 20-ounce can blueberry pie
  filling

Topping

One 8-ounce package cream cheese,
  at room temperature

One 8-ounce container sour cream

$^1/_2$ cup sugar

1 teaspoon vanilla extract

$^1/_2$ cup chopped pecans or walnuts

To prepare the Jell-O mixture, place the Jell-O in a large bowl with 2 cups boiling water. Let the Jell-O dissolve, and add the pineapple and pie filling. Pour into an oblong dish about 7 by 11 inches. Cover with plastic, place in the refrigerator, and chill until very firm.

To prepare the topping, cream together the cream cheese, sour cream, sugar, and vanilla using an electric mixer. Spread the topping over the Jell-O after it has firmed up. Sprinkle with the nuts and chill for at least 1 hour before serving.

Serves 6

Corn Pudding

Recipe from the kitchen of Ms. Bernice King

I began attending Abyssinian Baptist Church, the church home of my oldest daughter, Betty Ann Syphrette, when I decided that I needed to find a church closer to my home. After attending regularly for about three years, I became a member in 2003. I remember that twenty-three others joined the church the same Sunday that I did.

I don't do much cooking anymore, but every once in a while, someone in my family of five living children, six grandchildren, and three great-grandchildren will request this dish, or I, myself, get a taste and I "make me a corn puddin'."

Fresh-cut corn kernels are an important ingredient in this recipe, as fresh corn, taken straight from the cob, is more tender and juicy than corn from a can.

4 tablespoons unsalted butter, melted	$1/2$ teaspoon salt
2 cups fresh-cut corn kernels	1 teaspoon ground cinnamon
3 large eggs, lightly beaten	2 tablespoons vanilla extract
2 cups evaporated milk, warmed	2 tablespoons all-purpose flour or
$1^1/2$ cups sugar	cornstarch

Preheat the oven to 350°F. Butter an 8 by 8-inch casserole.

Combine all the ingredients in a large bowl. Pour into the casserole and place in a larger pan filled with hot water to cover 1 inch of the casserole dish. Bake for 45 minutes, or until pudding is heated through and begins to firm.

Serves 4 to 6

Homemade Granola

Recipe from the kitchen of Carole Darden-Lloyd

Once you realize how easy it is to make this cereal, you'll always want to have it on hand. It's listed as a dessert because it's great sprinkled over ice cream, but served for breakfast with low-fat milk or soymilk, it's a good way to start the day. You can vary the recipe by using grains and dried fruits of your choice. It can be stored in an airtight container for up to one month.

4 cups rolled oats

2 teaspoons ground cinnamon

$1^2/_3$ cups sliced almonds

6 tablespoons wheat germ

$^1/_3$ cup canola oil

$^1/_3$ cup honey

2 teaspoons vanilla extract

1 cup dried cranberries or other dried
 fruit of your choice

Preheat the oven to 325°F.

Combine the oats, cinnamon, almonds, and wheat germ in a large bowl. Combine the oil, honey, and vanilla in a small bowl. Pour the honey mixture over the oat mixture and stir until well combined. Line 2 cookie sheets with foil. Spread the mixture evenly on the cookie sheets. Bake for 10 minutes, then stir and bake for 5 minutes longer, or until golden. Remove from the oven and stir in the dried fruit while still hot. Let cool before serving.

Makes 7 to 8 cups

"Mommy's" Pineapple Upside-Down Cake in a Skillet

Recipe from the kitchen of Myrna Sanders

Cake

2¹/₂ cups all-purpose flour

1 tablespoon baking powder

¹/₄ cup (¹/₂ stick) unsalted butter or
  margarine

1¹/₂ cups sugar

1 tablespoon vanilla extract

2 large eggs

1 cup milk

Topping

¹/₄ cup (¹/₂ stick) plus 2 tablespoons
  unsalted butter or margarine

1 cup brown sugar

One 15-ounce can sweetened
  pineapple slices

One 6-ounce jar maraschino cherries,
  drained and stems removed

Preheat the oven to 350°F.

Sift the flour and baking powder into a medium bowl and set aside. Cream together the butter, sugar, vanilla, and eggs with an electric mixer. Add the dry ingredients to the wet, alternating with the milk, and mix well after each addition.

For the topping, melt the butter or margarine in a 10-inch cast-iron skillet over medium-high heat. Remove from the heat and sprinkle the brown sugar over the butter. Arrange the pineapple slices in the pan, placing cherries in the center of each pineapple slice. Spoon the batter into the skillet. Bake for 30 to 40 minutes, or until the center is set. Cool in pan for 10 minutes, then invert onto a plate. Serve warm.

Serves 6 to 8

Banana "Ice Cream"

Recipe from the kitchen of Carole Darden-Lloyd

This satisfying dessert is so rich and creamy, it's hard to believe that it's only ingredient is a banana. It should be consumed immediately since it does not re-freeze well.

1 ripe but not soft banana, peeled and
    sliced ¼-inch thick

Place the banana slices in a single layer in a zip-top bag. Freeze for several hours or overnight.

    Place the banana in a blender and pulse until smooth, scraping down the sides as needed.

Serves 1

The Oatmeal Cookie

Recipe from the kitchen of Robert Gore

Many favorite recipes are handed from one generation to the next. Learning the food preparation from parents, grandparents, aunts, and uncles is a tradition in many families. Frequently I call my mother for guidance on all sorts of cooking projects. She loves to share her tips with me, and I love the fact that she seems to especially enjoy our food chats. I know this because after my phone cooking lessons, she'll often call one

Bob Gore.

of my four sisters to stir them up with comments like "I'm glad that at least one of my children shows an interest in learning what little I know about cooking." Recently I had the occasion to bake a batch for my sister and nephews visiting from Houston. While sampling the cookies they called Ma to comment that they were surprisingly good. The conversation came full circle when I confirmed that the much-talked-about recipe was the one she gave me.

My total cooking repertoire consists of five entrées and five desserts—all my mother's recipes. Those tasting my cooking inevitably smile when I attribute the recipe to my mother.

The oatmeal cookies are a particularly big hit. I send them out at holidays, as get-well gifts, and for housewarmings, birthdays, and any occasion where food is appreciated.

I made a batch for my fellow jurors serving on a trial in Brooklyn's Supreme Court. This little surprise treat served as a fun icebreaker between the sixteen men and women from different neighborhoods and diverse backgrounds. They were pleasantly surprised, and after sampling them they smiled and complimented Ma. It was a great way to start our deliberations.

Making these cookies, and the other recipes my mother taught me, is my way of keeping the family's spiritual connection strong.

1 cup (2 sticks) unsalted butter	2 tablespoons vanilla extract
1 cup dark brown sugar	1 teaspoon coconut extract (optional)
1 cup granulated sugar	2 eggs, well beaten
1^1/$_2$ cup all-purpose flour	4 cups quick-cooking oats
2 teaspoons baking soda	1^1/$_2$ cups raisins
^{1}/$_2$ teaspoon salt	2 cups lightly broken walnuts

Preheat the oven to 350°F.

Combine the butter, brown sugar, granulated sugar, flour, baking soda, salt, vanilla, and coconut extract (if using) in a large microwaveable bowl and microwave for 2 minutes until the butter is fully melted. Stir until well blended. Stir in the eggs. Add the oats 1 cup at a time. The consistency will be very thick and gooey. Add the raisins and nuts. Form 1-inch balls of dough with your hands and place on ungreased cookie sheets. Bake for 10 to 12 minutes, or until the edges are lightly browned.

Makes 2 to 2^1/$_2$ dozen cookies

Tips: To prevent the cookie dough from sticking to your hands, lightly oil your hands with cooking spray. Try baking one or two cookies and sample them before making the remainder. Vary the sizes to determine desired thickness. Shorter baking time will yield softer, moister cookies.

Oatmeal Cranberry Cookies

Recipe from the kitchen of Carole Darden-Lloyd

This delicious variation on an old favorite is fun to make with children. Just try not to eat too many.

1 cup rolled oats	$^1/_2$ teaspoon baking soda
1 large egg, lightly beaten	$^1/_2$ cup chopped walnuts
$^3/_4$ cup unbleached all-purpose flour	$^1/_2$ teaspoon vanilla extract
$^1/_2$ teaspoon salt	$^1/_2$ cup Smart Balance Spread, melted
$^1/_2$ cup packed light brown sugar	$^1/_2$ cup dried cranberries

Preheat the oven to 375°F. Grease 2 cookie sheets and set aside.

Combine all the ingredients in a large bowl and mix well.

Drop the batter by rounded spoonfuls 2 inches apart onto the cookie sheets. Bake 10 to 12 minutes, or until lightly browned. Immediately remove the cookies with a spatula to a wire rack to cool.

Makes 2 dozen

Easy Cookies

Recipe from the kitchen of Jared Garner

This recipe was created by Jared Garner when he was twelve years old. (See the Garner family story on page 47.)

1 cup oleo or unsalted butter

1 cup powdered sugar

2 cups all-purpose flour

1 teaspoon vanilla extract

1 teaspoon lemon extract

Preheat the oven to 350°F.

Cream the oleo and powdered sugar in a large bowl. Slowly add the flour and mix until well incorporated. Add the vanilla and lemon extracts. Place tablespoonfuls of the dough on ungreased cookie sheets and press them with a glass dipped in ice water. Bake for 8 to 10 minutes, or until edges turn slightly brown.

Makes 2 dozen

BOB GORE

Student recipe tester.

Blueberry Cobbler

Recipe from the kitchen of Mrs. Tommie Jean Clark and Tramel Garner

Sauce

4 cups fresh blueberries

2 tablespoons fresh lemon juice

1 cup sugar

1 tablespoon all-purpose flour

1 teaspoon ground nutmeg

Dumplings

2 cups biscuit mix

1 large egg, well beaten

$^1/_4$ cup sugar

$^2/_3$ cup light cream

Zest of 1 orange

Whipped cream or ice cream, for serving

Combine the blueberries, lemon juice, sugar, flour, nutmeg, and 1 cup of water in a deep 10-inch skillet with a lid. Bring to a boil over high heat, reduce the heat, and simmer for 5 minutes, stirring frequently.

To make the dumplings, combine all the dumpling ingredients to form a soft dough. Drop the mixture by spoonfuls on top of the hot blueberries. Cover tightly and simmer for 20 minutes, or until the dumplings are firm and cooked through. Serve warm, topped with whipped cream or ice cream.

Serves 6

Carolina Marble Pound Cake

Recipe from the kitchen of Anitra Jones

This recipe was originally passed down to me as a basic pound cake recipe from my Aunt Louise of Lincolnton, North Carolina, my hometown. From about the age of ten years old, I enjoyed following adult family members into the kitchen to watch, listen, and help as they prepared delicious traditional Southern dishes—especially desserts made from scratch. When my Aunt Louise shared her special pound cake recipe with me, I remember being not at all intimidated to make the recipe all by myself, because the cake did not call for frosting. My mom, who is also a great cook, did not hesitate to give me my first rave reviews on how tasty and moist my first pound cake turned out. I beamed from the accolades that Mom poured out.

It has now been more than twenty years since I baked my first cake. Since then I have put my own twist on Aunt Louise's recipe, adding a chocolate swirl to give the cake a little mystery once sliced. I have made many, many desserts for family, friends, and loved ones. My love for making people smile by sharing wonderful sweets recently led me to start my own baking business called Aunt Ni Ni's Kitchen. I pray that my kitchen will exude the warmth and love that were so deeply a part of my childhood memories so that a young person is touched and inspired to continue this awesome legacy of sharing these Southern desserts. In addition to being a member of Abyssinian Baptist Church, I am involved also with the Blue Nile Passage, Inc., a not-for-profit mentoring program for teenage youth run completely by volunteers.

1 cup (2 sticks) unsalted butter

1 cup (2 sticks) margarine

3 cups sugar

5 large eggs

1 teaspoon vanilla extract

3 cups all-purpose flour, sifted

$^1/_2$ tablespoon baking powder

$^1/_4$ teaspoon salt

1 cup milk

$^1/_2$ cup unsweetened cocoa, sifted

Preheat the oven to 350°F. Grease and flour a 10-inch tube pan and set aside.

Combine the butter, margarine, and sugar in the large bowl of an electric mixer and beat at medium speed until creamy, 1 to 2 minutes. Add the eggs one at a time. Add the vanilla and mix another minute. Combine the flour, baking powder, and salt in a large bowl. Reduce the mixer speed to low. Add the flour mixture to the egg mixture alternately with milk. Mix just until blended, 1 to 2 minutes. Remove about 2 cups of the batter to a medium bowl and add the cocoa. Mix well. Spoon half of the plain batter into the prepared pan, then add half of the chocolate batter on top. Swirl the chocolate batter with the plain batter with a knife. Top with the remaining plain batter and spoon the remaining chocolate batter on top and swirl with a knife again. Bake for 1 hour and 15 minutes, or until a toothpick inserted in the center comes out clean. Cool for 15 minutes, then remove from the pan and cool completely on a wire rack.

Makes one 10-inch pound cake

Luscious Pound Cake

Recipe from the kitchen of Dorothy Nell Johnson

1¹/₂ cups (3 sticks) unsalted butter, room temperature	3 cups all-purpose flour
3 cups sugar	¹/₂ tablespoon baking powder
8-ounce package cream cheese, softened	1 cup heavy whipping cream
5 large eggs	1 teaspoon lemon or lime extract
	1 teaspoon vanilla extract

Preheat the oven to 325°F. Grease and flour a 10-inch Bundt pan and set aside.

Cream the butter, sugar, and cream cheese together in the large bowl of an electric mixer until fluffy. Add the eggs one at a time. Sift the flour and baking powder into a medium bowl. Alternately add the flour and the whipping cream to the butter mixture. Add the lemon and vanilla extracts to the batter and mix well. Pour the batter into the prepared pan and bake for about 2 hours, or until a toothpick inserted into the center comes out clean, or the top springs back slightly when gently pressed. The sides of the cake will also draw away from the sides of the pan when the cake is done.

Serves 8 to 10

Apple Pie

Recipe from the kitchen of Jewel Thompson

4 medium McIntosh or other cooking
   apples
2 tablespoons cooking sherry
Scant $^3/_4$ cup sugar
2 tablespoons cornstarch

$^3/_4$ teaspoon apple pie spice
One 9-inch unbaked ready-made
   pastry with top
2 tablespoons melted unsalted butter
   or margarine

Preheat the oven to 375°F.

Peel, core, and slice the apples. Place in a large bowl and pour the sherry over the apple slices. Stir to cover all the pieces. Combine the sugar, cornstarch, and apple pie spice in a small bowl. Add to the apples and toss to coat. Pour the mixture into the prepared pie crust and pour the melted butter evenly over the apples. Make a lattice-top crust by cutting the top crust into 8 strips. Place 4 of the strips across the pie, spacing them evenly. Place the 4 remaining strips across the first 4 strips, weaving the strips in and out. Trim the edges and cover with foil. Bake for 25 minutes, then remove the foil and bake another 20 to 25 minutes, or until the top is golden and the fruit is tender.

Serves 8

Beverages

Blueberry Lemonade

Recipe from the kitchen of Verna Rose Martin

Blueberries are one of the healthiest berries on the planet you can eat (or drink!). They're packed with nutrients.

2 cups fresh blueberries
Juice of 6 lemons

Brown sugar to taste
Lemon slices, for garnish

Place the blueberries and 4 cups water in a blender and puree. Strain into a large jug. Add another 4 cups water to the jug, along with the lemon juice and brown sugar. Stir vigorously. Serve on ice with lemon slices.

Makes about 2 quarts

Carrot Juice

BOB GORE

Recipe from the kitchen of the late Manasseh Gordon

This drink must be consumed the same day it's made.

Manasseh Gordon.

2 pounds carrots chopped, about
   8 to 10
One 14-ounce can condensed milk

1 teaspoon vanilla extract
2 tablespoons fresh lime or lemon
   juice

Place the carrots in a blender along with 4 cups water. Blend on low speed, then strain into a pitcher. Add the condensed milk, vanilla, and lime juice and stir to combine. Serve immediately.

Makes about 5 cups

Variation: You can also make carrot juice simply by passing carrots, along with some apple pieces, through a juicer.

Homemade Peach Wine

Recipe from the kitchen of Deborah Willis Kennedy

My mom's grandmother, Catherine Foreman, known to us as Mom Foreman, made peach pies and sent her children and grandchildren out to sell them for five cents at the subway stop at Broad Street and Columbia Avenue in North Philadelphia. They sold pies on Friday and Saturday nights and families often told them that the pies were served on Sunday for dessert. The leftover peaches and peach skins were used to make peach wine, which was served during the winter holidays.

This is a three-month process. Start in August and finish in November for a nice treat for the holidays.

1 pound peaches   One 6-ounce yeast cake
2 cups sugar

Combine the peaches in a large glass jug or pot with a tight lid. Add the sugar, 12 cups water, and yeast cake. Cover. Place in a cool, dark place for 3 weeks. Pour through a cheesecloth-lined strainer into a clean container. Pour the wine into 2 glass gallon bottles. Cover and return to the cool, dark place for another 9 weeks.

Makes 2 gallons

Berry Smoothie

(from www.blackvegetarians.com)

Recipe from the kitchen of Mrs. Earnestine Adams,
CFO, choir member, deaconess

This recipe was provided to the many Abyssinian members who participated in the church's recent weight-loss challenge.

$^1/_2$ 10 ounce package frozen mixed berries

$^1/_2$ cup water or soy, almond, or rice milk

3 ripe bananas, peeled, chopped, and frozen

2 dates

Place all the ingredients in a blender and blend at high speed until smooth. Serve immediately.

Serves 2

Fruit Smoothie

Recipe from the kitchen of Carole Darden-Lloyd

While whole fresh frozen berries are available in supermarkets, it is easy to prepare your own during peak berry season. Place whole fresh berries in a single
layer on a cookie sheet and freeze. Once frozen, place in a zip-top bag and store
in the freezer until ready to use.

2 cups ice cubes

1 cup papaya or mango nectar

$^3/_4$ cup unsweetened pineapple
  juice

$^1/_2$ ripe banana

$^1/_3$ cup fresh frozen blackberries,
  raspberries, strawberries, or
  blueberries

$^1/_2$ cup plain low-fat or nonfat yogurt

1 tablespoon honey

Place all the ingredients in a blender and blend until smooth. Serve immediately.

Serves 4 to 6

Very Berry Clean and Delicious Blend

Recipe from the kitchen of Fay Daley

6 to 8 fresh strawberries

1 cup fresh raspberries

1 cup fresh blueberries

$1/4$ cup water

1 tablespoon fresh lemon juice

Place all the berries along with $1/4$ cup water in a blender and blend until smooth. Add the lemon juice. Strain and serve over crushed ice, if desired.

Serves 2

Summertime Punch

Recipe from the kitchen of C. Vernon Mason

This recipe evolved over a period of years from our Annual Deacon, Deaconess, and Trustee Picnics.

1 quart cranberry juice

1 quart orange juice

1 quart apple juice

$^1/_2$ large can Country Time Lemonade
   Mix

1 quart ginger ale

5 pounds ice

Lime, lemon, orange, and apple slices,
   for serving

Combine the juices, lemonade mix, and ginger ale in a large pot. Stir well. Add the ice and top with the fruit slices. Serve in 8-ounce cups over crushed ice.

Makes 1 gallon

Chai

Recipe from the kitchen of Dr. Anita Underwood (Originated from Siddha Yoga Meditation ashrams)

The word *chai* means "tea" in the Hindi language. Beginning in the early 1970s, Swami Muktananda offered chai to the students in his ashram in India before the *Guru Gita* recitation. Now chai is served with breakfast in Siddha Yoga Meditation ashrams.

4 whole cloves

4 cardamon pods, crushed

1 cinnamon stick

Four $1/4$-inch-thick slices fresh ginger

1 tablespoon Earl Grey tea leaves

1 tablespoon Darjeeling tea leaves

1 cup soymilk

2 tablespoons honey

Bring $3^1/4$ cups water to a boil in a medium pot. Add the cloves, cardamon, cinnamon, and ginger. Cover, reduce the heat to low, and simmer for 5 minutes. Turn off the heat and add the tea leaves. Steep for 3 minutes. Heat the milk in a small pot over medium heat until almost boiling. Strain the chai through a fine-mesh strainer into a warmed teapot. Stir in the hot milk and sugar and serve immediately.

Serves 4

Power Protein Shake

Recipe from the kitchen of Dr. Anita Underwood

1 cup unsweetened cranberry or apple
   juice

$^1/_3$ frozen banana

5 fresh blueberries

2 scoops protein powder

Place all the ingredients in a blender and blend until smooth. Serve immediately.

Serves 1

Aggressively Planning for Good Health: Some Healthful Suggestions

Limit Your Intake of Prepared Foods

Canned, frozen, or packaged foods are frequently overprocessed and contain more sugar and salt than vitamins and minerals. If a product has a list of ingredients impossible to pronounce, these may be chemical additives that you should do without. These additives may enhance the texture, taste, or shelf life of a food, but they are counterproductive to good health. There is, in fact, a direct link between overprocessed foods and today's most common health concerns such as diabetes, high blood pressure, and obesity.

If the food industry itself is conspiring against you, what should you eat? As a general rule, increase your fiber intake, as fiber protects against excess fats. This means eating more grains, beans, root crops, vegetables, and fruits. Treat fried foods, red meat, white bread, and other products made from refined flour as a delicacy to be eaten sparingly. In choosing snacks, think fruit, nuts, seeds, or popcorn (that you've popped yourself). In short, select foods that are as close to nature and God's original intention as possible.

Read Labels

There is nothing more important than understanding how the food you eat directly affects your health. Begin by reading the nutritional labels on the cans and boxes of food in your own cabinets. Any product that contains partially hydrogenated or hydrogenated oils and/or high fructose corn syrup should be considered a danger to your health.

Hydrogenated oils are the major source of trans fats, which have been linked to cancer and have been found to raise the bad kind of cholesterol, called LDL, and to lower HDL, the good kind. Simply put, they can cause heart disease. According to studies done by Harvard Medical School, for every four to five grams of trans fat you consume, your risk of heart disease nearly doubles. It is estimated that on average Americans consume five to six grams of trans fats daily. High fructose corn syrup is an ingredient in nearly all prepared snack foods. It has replaced sugar as a sweetener because an overproduction of corn has made it a very inexpensive by-product. But scientists now feel that the increasingly high incidence of type 2 diabetes and obesity in Americans, especially children, is due to the manner in which high fructose corn syrup is processed by the body.

A visit to your food cabinets and refrigerator will show you how pervasive hydrogenated fats and high fructose corn syrup are. You'll find them in pancake mixes, microwave popcorn, cake frostings, and breads, to name a few. Now that you are armed with this information, your next trip to the grocery store can be a thoughtful one where you choose products that have your health foremost in mind. Determine to know as much as you can about what is good for you and what is not. The information is there—be informed.

Visit Health Food Stores

Familiarize yourself with natural, unrefined products. Consider organic produce, particularly as a substitute for fruits and vegetables that are high in pesticides such as strawberries, bell peppers, spinach, cherries, peaches, celery, apples, green beans, and cucumbers. Organic produce can be more expensive, so if it just isn't in your budget, make certain to wash all produce thoroughly and consider using a vegetable and fruit wash, available in many grocery stores.

Think Beyond Soul Food

An occasional visit to the cuisine of other cultures can give you an appreciation of different types of food and show you how other countries do not rely on prepared, processed foods to the extent that this country does. It can also give you ideas on how to prepare your own culture's food in a more healthful way.

Read Books and Magazines That Promote Healthy Lifestyles

Many magazines, books, and websites are filled with helpful information and ideas about healthy food preparation. Experiment with new recipes. It adds a sense of adventure and lessens the drudgery that can be part of time spent hovering over a hot stove. Inspire yourself and your family by trying a new recipe once a week, or at least once a month.

Cook with Your Children

Educate your children about food and nutrition. Make cooking a recreational activity that gives them an investment in their own health. According to a 2001 study published in the *Journal of Nutrition Education,* the average child in the United States will watch nearly ten thousand commercials touting food or beverages a year. One result of this is an overconsumption of soda. Once made with sugar, soda is now made almost entirely with high fructose corn syrup, as are most prepared snacks. Diet soda is not the answer, since we now have data showing that sugar substitutes can actually trick the body into thinking that it needs to consume more calories. Carbonated drinks also contain high levels of phosphates, which encourage the kidneys to eliminate calcium. Doctors now suspect a strong correlation between high consumption of soda during stages of bone development in children and the high incidence of osteoporosis in this country. Armed with this information, what decisions will you and your child make regarding how often soda and other such products are consumed?

Count Calories

Anything you eat beyond your immediate need for energy turns to fat, whether it comes from fat, protein, or carbohydrates. The government recommends 1,600 calories a day for the average sedentary woman and 2,200 for men. Analyze your caloric intake and gradually reduce unnecessary foods—those with empty calories and no nutritional benefit.

Get Moving

There are few things more satisfying than finding an activity you enjoy and sticking to it. If working out seems too much like work to you and something to be dreaded, then you haven't found the right match, or perhaps your goal is too high, more than you are in shape to reach. Start small and keep the enjoyment level high. As you gain in endurance and strength, you can always add a block to your walk, an extra lap to your swim, or ten minutes to an aerobic workout. Try to build up to thirty minutes at least five times a week. Our own Health Ministry is offering wonderful exercise classes. If you can't get there, start your own group or join the YMCA. Rhythmic movement is part of your heritage. If you've lost it, you can recapture it.

Honor Your Ancestors

Your genes carry with them an incredible history and are a part of you through the greatest of sacrifices. It is far from being a platitude when we say "only the strongest survived." Millions died on the route from capture to forced treks across land, to the dark, dank coastal slave castles through the abject misery of the middle passage, to three hundred years of enslavement in which your ancestors endured poor food and shelter, little clothing, and sun-up to sun-down back-breaking work. A strong body is your natural heritage. Revere this remarkable genealogical path by taking loving, thoughtful care of your physical self. Your spiritual self will be forever indebted.

—Carole Darden-Lloyd

Project Team Bios

ROSCOE BETSILL, our food stylist, works as a food stylist, tabletop prop stylist, writer, and recipe developer. He earned a Grand Diplôme from LaVarenne École de Cuisine in Paris. His clients include *Metropolitan Home, Oprah, Bon Appétit, Food & Wine, Gourmet, House Beautiful, Good Housekeeping,* and *Essence* magazines, as well as Kraft Foods, General Mills, Atkins, M&M Mars, Viking Kitchens, Ruby Tuesday, and Outback Steakhouse.

ZANA BILLUE, our recipe tester, is president and founder of Zana Cakes, Inc., a mail-order pound cake company located in Philadelphia. Zana received a full-tuition scholarship to and is a graduate of the Culinary Institute of America in Hyde Park, New York. She has worked as a recipe development specialist for Nestlé USA, concept development chef for ARAMARK, and consultant for Campbell Soup Company.

WILLIAM BOYD, our photographer, is a New York–based commercial and fine arts photographer. He was born and raised in Philadelphia and studied engineering at North Carolina A&T University and North Carolina State University and photography at the University of the Arts in Philadelphia. His clients include *Town & Country, Metropolitan Home, This Old House,* and *Essence* magazines.

TONYA HOPKINS, our recipe collector, is a contributing researcher and writer for the *Encyclopedia of American Food and Drink* (Oxford University Press, 2004) and the founder of THoughtCo: Commentary on Things Culinary and Cultural. She has written for *Essence, Food Forum Quarterly,* and *Food History News* on topics including food and wine pairing, food and culture, slavery and rum, and African influences on foods in the Americas. She is a graduate of the University of Pennsylvania and lives in Brooklyn.

ADRIENNE INGRUM, our project manager, has twenty-five years of experience in book publishing. She has served as vice president at G. P. Putnam's & Sons (now part of the Penguin Group), Waldenbooks, and Crown, a division of Random House, publishing more than five hundred fiction, nonfiction, and sideline titles and working with scores of authors. Ingrum has been an independent publishing consultant for the past ten years. She launched and oversees *Black Issues Book Review,* served as lead consultant for Doubleday Direct (now Bookspan) in the development of the Black Expressions Book Club, and has consulted for corporations such as Urban Ministries, Inc., the largest African American Christian publisher.

BOOKER T. MATTISON, our writer, is an award-winning writer and director whose films and music videos have screened extensively in the United States and Europe. His film adaptation of *The Gilded Six Bits,* based on the Zora Neale Hurston short story, was televised nationally on the Showtime cable network's ninth annual Black Filmmaker Showcase. It was rated as the best of the films featured by the *Hollywood Reporter.* Mattison's films have screened at the Smithsonian Institution and the Library of Congress in Washington, D.C., the Directors Guild of America in Hollywood, and Harvard University. Abroad his work has been showcased on the television show *Sanostra* in Madrid and MTV Europe. His music video for the Cross Movement's song "Know Me" was in rotation on Black Entertainment Television, the Trinity Broadcasting Network, and the Word Network. He has served as a reviewer of written works on film for *Black Issues Book Review* magazine. He recently wrote and directed the Cross Movement's music video for the song "When I Flow" from their latest album, Holy Culture, which is currently the fastest selling Gospel hip-hop album in history.

Mattison was featured as "a filmmaker on the verge" in *Vibe* magazine. His work also has been discussed in the *Christian Science Monitor, Black Issues Book Review,* and *Feed* magazines. He has received the prestigious Warner Brothers Pictures Production Award, the *Entertainment Weekly* Post-Production Award, and a Spike Lee Fellowship. He has taught film production at Brooklyn College, Literary Criticism at the College of New Rochelle, and apologetics at Tabernacle Bible Institute. He received a bachelor of science in mass communications from Norfolk State University and a Master of Fine Arts in film from New York University.

STUDENT RECIPE TESTERS Tah'swanna Khali Davis and Tiani Watson participate in the C-Cap Program, which encourages young people of color to enter culinary professions.

RECIPE TESTERS John Gamble-Jennings and Quiyona Gould are high school students who aspire to culinary careers and attend the Harlem Tabernacle Church of New York City.

Index

Grateful acknowledgment is made to the following for permission to reprint previously published material:

Kraft Foods, Inc.: "Original GERMANS® Sweet Chocolate Cake and Coconut-Pecan Filling and Frosting" recipes. BAKER'S®, GERMAN'S®, ANGEL FLAKE® and PLANTERS® are registered trademarks of KF Holdings. Reprinted courtesy of KRAFT KITCHEN®, Kraft Foods, Inc.

Sylvia Woods: "Smothered Chicken Recipe" from *Sylvia's Soul Food: Recipes from Harlem's World-Famous Restaurant* by Sylvia Woods and Christopher Styler, copyright © 1992 by Sylvia Woods (Heart Books, 1992). Reprinted by permission of the author.

"Cotton pickers" (p. viii) courtesy of General Research & Reference Division, Schomberg Center for Research in Black Culture, The New York Public Library, Astor, Lenox and Tilden Foundations.

About the Type

The text of this book is set in Loire, which was created by the French type designer Jean Lochu. In 1968, Lochu met Albert Hollenstein, who recognized Lochu's talent and gave him the opportunity to design his own typefaces at Hollenstein Studios, where, ever since, he has been creating original fonts especially suited for elegant text typography. Lochu, whose training as a designer is rooted in the classical tradition, is said to have designed the Loire typeface "with the Garamond spirit."